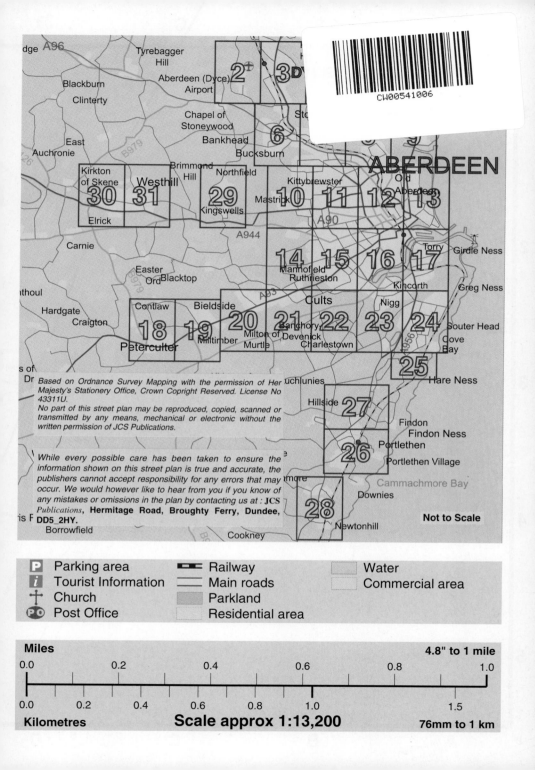

CW00541006

Miles

4.8" to 1 mile

| 0.0 | 0.2 | 0.4 | 0.6 | 0.8 | 1.0 |

Kilometres

Scale approx 1:13,200

76mm to 1 km

| 0.0 | 0.2 | 0.4 | 0.6 | 0.8 | 1.0 | 1.5 |

P Parking area
i Tourist Information
✝ Church
PO Post Office

▭▭ Railway
━━ Main roads
▨ Parkland
▢ Residential area

▨ Water
▢ Commercial area

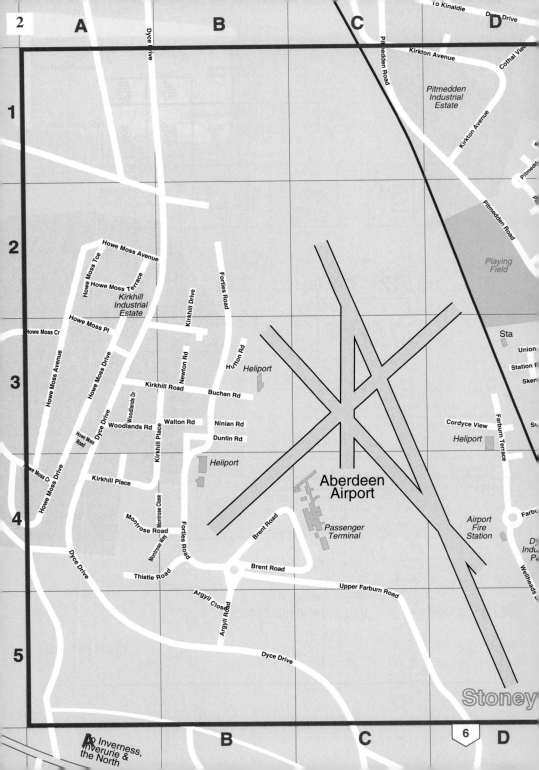

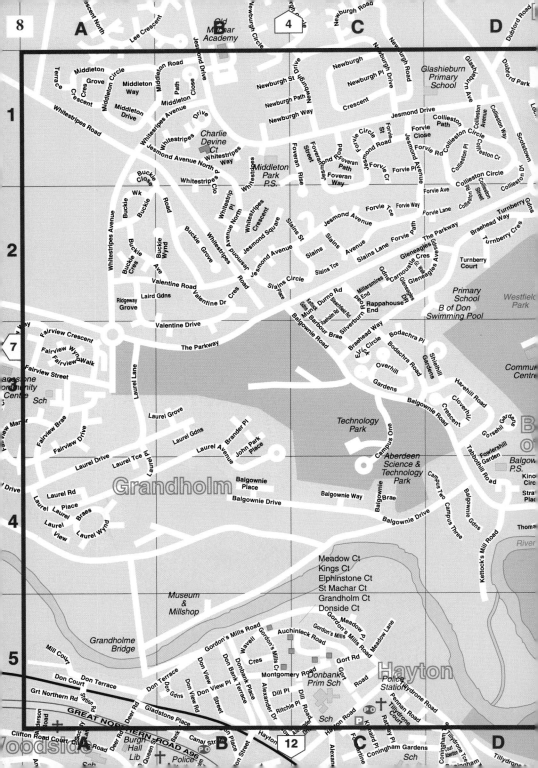

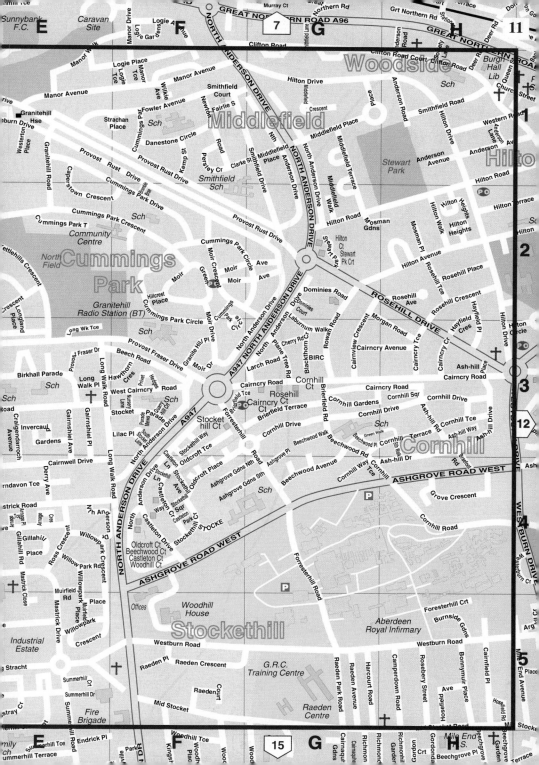

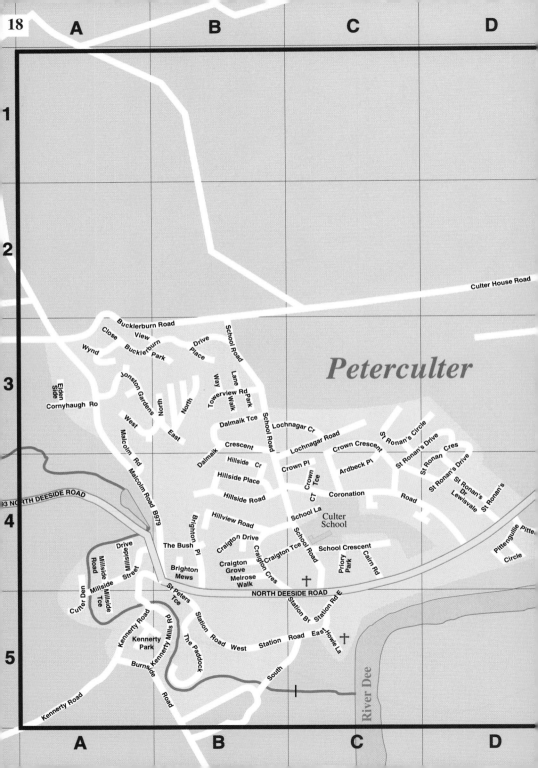

18

A B C D

1

2

Culter House Road

Peterculter

Bucklerburn Road
View
Close Bucklerburn
Wynd Park Drive
School Road Place

3

Elden Side
Cornyhaugh Ro
Jonston Gardens
West
Malcolm Rd
North
North
East
Way
Lane
Towerview Rd
Walk
Park
Dalmaik Tce
School Road
Lochnagar Cr
Lochnagar Road
St Ronan's Circle
St Ronan's Drive
Cres
Dalmaik Crescent
Crown Crescent
St Ronan
Hillside Cr
Crown Pl
Ardbeck Pl
St Ronan's Drive
St Ronan's Drive
Hillside Place
Crown
CT Tce
Coronation
St Ronan's
Lewisvale
St Ronan's
Malcolm Road B979
Hillside Road
CT Tce
Road

93 NORTH DEESIDE ROAD

4

Brighton Pl
Hillview Road
School La
Culter School
Pittengullie Pitte
Drive
The Bush
Craigton Drive
Craigton Tce
School Road
Pittengullie
Millside Road
Drepsillim
Street
Brighton
Mews
Craigton Grove
Craigton Cres
Craigton Tce
School Crescent
Priory Park
Cairn Rd
Circle
Melrose Walk
Culter Den
Millside Tce
Millside
St Peters Tce
NORTH DEESIDE ROAD
Station Br
Station Rd E

5

Kennerty Road
Kennerty Park
Kennerty Mills Rd
The Paddock
Station Road West
Station Road East
Howie La
Burnside
Road
South

River Dee

Kennerty Road

A B C D

Contlaw Road

Binghill Road

Oldfold Pl

Oldfold Park

Oldfold Ave

Oldfold Walk

The Meadows

Oldfold Dr

Oldfold Cres

Binghill Hed

Tor-Na-Dee Hospital

Colthill Cres

Colthill Road

Binghill Drive

Binghill Road North

Binghill Road West

Colthill Circle

Colthill Dr

Colthill Circle

Contlaw Road

Colthill Circle

Contlaw Place

Contlaw Brae

Braehead Tce

Binghill Crescent

Binghill Park

Contlaw Brae

Monearn Gardens

Milltimber P.S.

Binghill Road

NORTH DEESIDE ROAD A93

Beaconhill R

Bea
onhill

Sune

Culter House Road

Bellenden Walk

Robertson

NORTH DEESIDE ROAD

American School

Station Rd East

Milltimbe

Brae

B979

Station Road

Murtle Den Road

Milltimber

Camphill School

River Dee

SOUTH DEESIDE ROAD B9077

B979

B9077 South Deeside Road

1

2

3

20

4

5

A   B   C   D

1

Cults Burn

2

Public Park

Baillieswells Road

Cults P.S.

Pinecrest Drive

Pinecrest Walk

Pinecrest Circle

Pinecrest Gdns

Circle

Way

Dalmunzie Road

Springdale Road

Springdale Crescent

Baillieswells Grove

Place

Court

Park

Earlspark Crescent

Earlsp Gardens

Earlspark

Earlspark Avenue

Earlspark Road

Earls Drive

Earlspark Drive

Earlswells View

Earlswells Road

Earlswells Dr

Earlswells Place

EARLSWEL

Cairnlee Cr Nth

Cairnlee Cr Sth

Cairnlee Road

Cairnlee Avenue East

Cairnside

Craig Gdns

Cairn Cres

Cairn Park

Cairn Walk

Manse Road

Cairn Ga

3

Baillieswells

Crescent

Baillieswells Place

Cairnlee Tce

Cairnlee Park

Baillieswells Road

Cairn Road

Cairn Road

Murtleden Road

Hillhead Road

Murtle Dam

Dalmunzie Road

Baillieswells Terrace

Baillieswell Drive

Prospecthill Rd

Gowanbrae Road

Bieldside Sth Rd

Golfview Road

4

Marchbank Road

Golf Road

Old Ferry Road

Deeside Golf Co

5

To Milltimber

A93 NORTH DEESIDE ROAD

Sunert Rd

Beaconhill

A   B   C   D

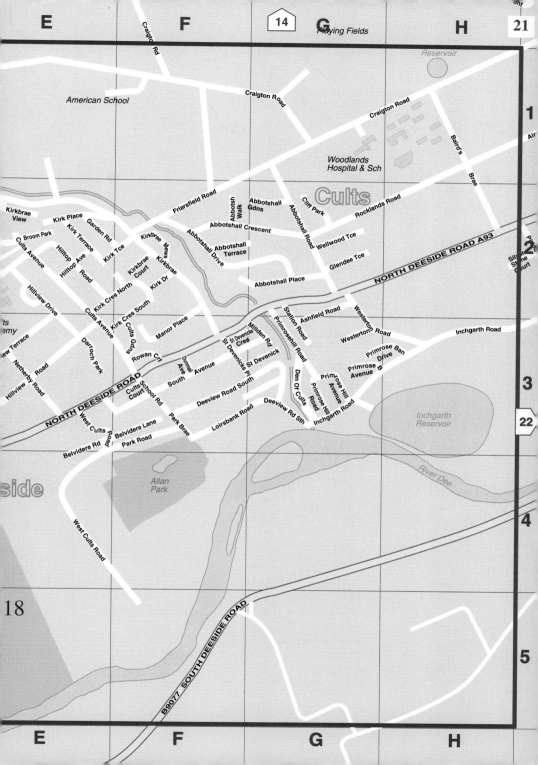

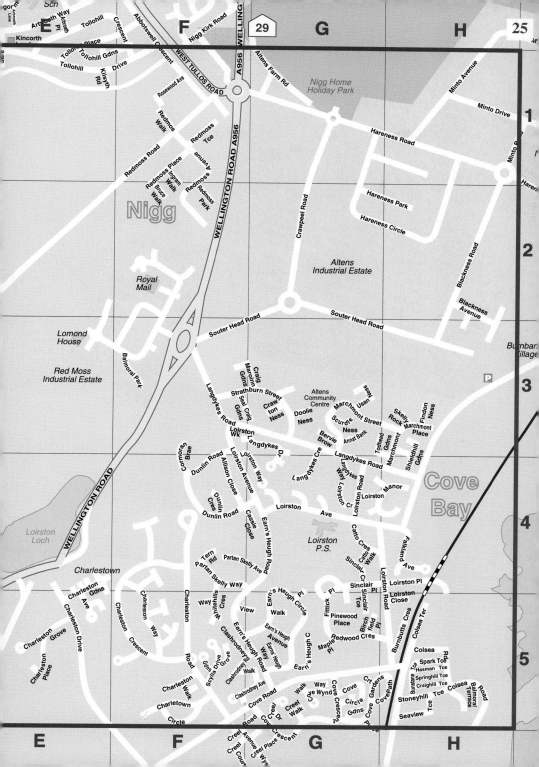

Portlethen

A B C D

1

2

3

4

5

Boswell Road
Boswell Walk
Boswell Avenue
Boswell
Boswell Way
Boswell Road
Boswell Wynd

Clashfarq Cres
Craighead
Broomfield Park
Cairnwell Drive
Avenue
MUIREND ROAD
Willow Wynd
Whinpark Circle
Mosside Cres
Fern Drive
Fern Place

Smithy

Alder Drive
Alder Drive
Gorse Circle
Berrymuir Wynd
Berrymuir Road
Eastsyde Pl
BRUNTLAND ROAD
Broomfield
Myrtle Terrace
Juniper Place
Sedge Road
Place
Marsh Place

Drumwacket Drive
Bourtree Ave
Circle
Cairngrassie Circle
Cairngrassie Drive
Cammach
Berrymuir Place
Lethen Walk
Easter Court
Easter Drive
Easter Drive
Easter Place
Ash Ct
The Green
Ash Place
Berrymuir Road
Ash Grove
Aspen Way
Acorn Place
Oak Drive

Pav
Community Centre
Fishermoss PS
Portlethen Academy
Swimming Pool
Oak Drive
Bruntland Court
Bruntland Cour
BRUNTLAND ROAD

Baganlochie Road
Downies Road

Longhillock Cotts
Lochside

Mains of Clashfarquhar

Seacroft

A B C D

1

2

3

4

5

Portlethen
Golf Course

18

Badentoy Road

Hotel

Schoolhill Road

Mosside Drive

MUIREND ROAD

Dunvegan Place

Glascairn Avenue

vegan Avenue

Glascairn Pl

Rowanbank Road

Glebe Ct

COOKSTON ROAD

Cookston Cotts

Barclayhill Place

Thistle Drive

Piper Place

Claymore Avenue

Viking Place

Ninian Place

Road

Nicol Place

Burnside Gdns

Devenick Drive

Hillsdale Terrace

Heather Place

ace

The Square

Liby

Portlethen PS

Police Station

Argyll Place

Community Centre

†

Medical Centre

Pond

Mill of Findon

Findon

A B C D

1

2

3

4

5

Hotel

Romsdal

Dunlukin

Cranhill

Burn of Elsick

St Anne's Cres

St Michael's Road

St Anne's Wynd

Bridge Croft

St John's Walk

St Michael's Road

St Michael's Cres

Elsick Mill

St Andrew's Tce

St Michael's Cres

St Michael's Way

Dunlin Ct

Plover Ct

Newtonhill Farm

St Michael's Walk

St Michael's Way

Turnstone Ct

Fulmar Ct

Tern Ct

St Nathan's Rd

St Michael's Pl

Sanderling Ct

Shore Cott

Puffin Ct

Newtonhill

St Peter's Road

Road

Mill Road

Newton

Newtonvale Ct

Newton Pl

Road

Cranhill

Murray Road

Newton Bay

Dran

Cranhill Brae

Craig Pl

Place

St Ternan's Road

St Crispin's Road

Elsick Pl

Whiteland Rd

Hillhead Croft

Bettridge Road

Skateraw Road

Greystone Pl

Hillhead Road

Chapel Rd

Head land Ct

Villagelands Rd

South Rd

Newtonhill Road

Playing Fields

Pav

Anderson Dr

Tel Exch

Cliff View

Crollshillock Pl

Newtonhill PS

Cliff View

Crollshillock Pl

Place

Berryhill Pl

CH

Community Centre

Cairnhill Rd

Park

Windyedge Ct

A90

Heathfield Park

A B C D

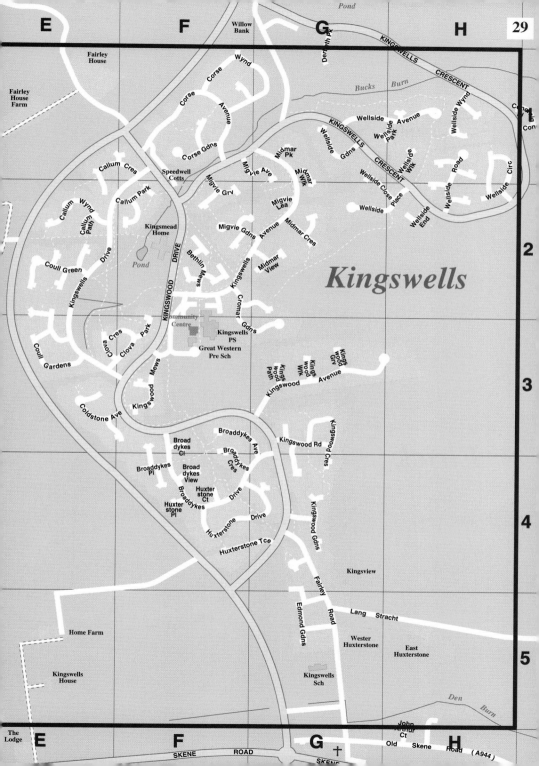

A　　**B**　　**C**　　**D**

Souterhill

1

Sunnybrae House

Berryhill

Loch View

Cairnie View

Westhill Heights

CH

Westhill Golf Course

18

2

Broadshade

Westhill Grange

Westhill Cres

Harvest Hill

Spring Tyne

Dunecht Gdns

HAY'S WAY

Keir Circle

Shaw Circle

Crombie PS

Fallow Rd

Lea Rig

Crombie Rd

Acres

Crombie Pl

Crombie Circ

Dunecht Road

Westwood Gr

West

Westwood Way

West

3

Old Skene Road

Clover Meadow

Crombie Dr

Crombie Wynd

Crombie Close

Leddach Rd

Leddach Pl

Leddach Gdns

Leslie Cres

Elrick

Larg Drive

Kirkton Rd

Kirkton Ave

Kirkton Gdns

Broadlands Gdns

Westdyke Cl Terrace

Westdyke Gardens

Blackhills Place

Blackhills Ct

Wellgrove Cres

Beechwood Pl

Beech Wood

Beechwood Gdns

Beechwood

Oak Cres

Hazel

Leddach Farmhouse

A944

Broadstraik Ave

Broadstraik Pl

Westdyke Ct

Westdyke Way

Westdyke Gardens

Westdyke Avenue

Blackhills Way

Westdyke Pl

Westdyke Walk

Leisure Centre

Wellgrove

Aspen Grove

Wellgrove Road

Elrick PS

Rowan Drive

4

Broadstraik Farm

Homelea

Westdyke Drive

Straik Place

The Courtyard

Fraser Drive

Wellgrove Dr

Henderson Drive

Brimmond La

Brimmond Way

Cruikshank Ct

STRAIK ROAD

5

Peregrine Road

Westhi Ind Es

A　　**B**　　**C**　　**D**

Street	Map	Grid
Abbey Rd.	17	G3
Abbey La.	17	G3
Abbey Pl.	17	G3
Abbey Sq.	17	G4
Abbots Pl.	23	G1
Abbotsford La.	16	D3
Abbotsford Pl.	16	D3
Abbotshall Cres.	21	F2
Abbotshall Dr.	21	F2
Abbotshall Gdns.	21	G2
Abbotshall Pl.	21	G2
Abbotshall Rd.	21	G2
Abbotshall Tce.	21	F2
Abbotshall Wk.	21	F2
Abbotswell Cres	23	D1
Abbotswell Dr.	23	F1
Abbotswell Rd.	23	D1
Abergeldie Rd.	16	B4
Abergeldie Tce.	16	B4
Aboyne Gdns.	22	D1
Aboyne Pl.	22	D2
Aboyne Rd.	22	C2
Academy St.	16	D2
Acorn Pl.	26	B4
Adelphi La.	16	D1
Adelphi.	16	D1
Advocates Rd.	12	D4
Affleck Pl.	16	D2
Affleck St.	16	D2
Airyhall Ave.	15	E5
Airyhall Cres.	14	D5
Airyhall Dr.	15	E5
Airyhall Gdns.	15	E5
Airyhall Pl.	15	E5
Airyhall Rd.	22	E1
Airyhall Tce.	15	E5
Albany Ct.	16	C2
Albert La.	16	A2
Albert Pl.	16	B1
Albert Quay.	17	F2
Albert St.	16	B1
Albert Tce.	16	B2
Albert Tce. Gdns.	16	B2
Albert Wk.	16	B2
Albury Pl.	16	C3
Albury Rd.	16	C3
Albyn Gro.	16	A2
Albyn La.	16	D2
Albyn Pl.	16	B2
Albyn Tce.	16	A2
Alder Dr.	26	A2
Alexander Dr.	8	B5
Alexander Tce.	12	B1
Alford Pl.	16	B2
Allan St.	16	B4
Allenvale Gdns.	16	B5
Allenvale Rd.	16	B5
Allison Cl.	25	E4
Alma Rd.	9	G3
Altens Farm Rd.	24	B3
Altonrea Gdns.	3	F3
Anderson Ave.	11	H1
Anderson Dr.	15	G3
Anderson Dr.	28	D4
Anderson La.	11	H1
Anderson Rd.	11	H1
Angusfield Ave.	15	E2
Angusfield La.	15	E2
Ann St.	12	B5
Annat Bank.	24	B5
Annfield Tce.	15	H3
Arbroath La.	23	D2
Arbroath Pl.	23	D2
Arbroath Way.	23	D2
Ardarroch Ct.	13	E3
Ardarroch Pl.	13	E3
Ardarroch Rd.	13	E3
Ardbeck Pl.	18	C4
Ardlair Tce.	3	F2
Argyll Cl.	2	B5
Argyll Cres.	12	A5
Argyll Pl.	12	A5
Argyll Pl.	27	G4
Argyll Rd.	2	B5
Arnage Cres.	11	E4
Arnage Dr.	10	D4
Arnage Gdns.	11	E4
Arnage Pl.	11	E4
Arnage Tce.	11	E4
Arnhall Cres.	31	G4
Arnhall Dr.	31	G4
Arran Ave.	10	B5
Aryburn Row.	3	E3
Aryburn Row.	3	E3
Ash Ct.	26	B3
Ash Gro.	26	B4
Ash Pl.	26	B3
Ash-Hill Dr.	11	H3
Ash-Hill Pl.	11	H3
Ash-Hill Rd.	11	H3
Ash-Hill Way.	11	H3
Ashdale Ct.	31	E4
Ashdale Ct.	31	F3
Ashdale Dr.	31	F3
Ashfield Rd.	21	G3
Ashgrove Ave.	12	B3
Ashgrove Ct.	12	B3
Ashgrove Gdns. N.	11	F4
Ashgrove Gdns. S.	11	F4
Ashgrove Pl.	11	G4
Ashgrove Rd.	12	A4
Ashgrove Rd. W.	11	H4
Ashley Gdns.	16	A3
Ashley Gro.	16	B3
Ashley La.	16	A3
Ashley Pk. Dr.	16	A3
Ashley Pk. N.	16	A3
Ashley Pk. S.	16	A3
Ashley Rd.	16	A3
Ashtown Pl.	6	B5
Ashtown Wk.	6	B5
Ashvale Ct.	16	B3
Ashvale Pl.	16	B3
Ashwood Cres.	4	B2
Ashwood Dr.	4	B1
Ashwood Gra.	4	B2
Ashwood Rd	4	B1
Aspen Gro.	30	C4
Aspen Way.	26	C4
Auchinleck Rd.	8	C5
Auchinyell Gdns.	22	D1
Auchinyell Rd.	22	D1
Auchinyell Tce.	22	D1
Auchlea Pl.	10	C5
Auchlea Rd.	10	C5
Auchlossan Ct.	9	E4
Auchmill Rd.	7	F5
Auchmill Tce.	7	F5
Auchriny Circ.	6	B1
Auldearn Gdns.	23	G2
Auldearn La.	23	G2
Auldearn Pl.	23	G2
Auldearn Rd.	23	G2
Aulton Ct.	13	E1
Avon Pl.	3	E3
Back Hilton Rd.	12	A3
Back Wynd.	16	D1
Badentoy Ave.	27	E1
Badentoy Cres.	27	E1
Baillieswells Cres.	20	C3
Baillieswells Dr.	20	C4
Baillieswells Gro.	20	B3
Baillieswells Pl.	20	C3
Baillieswells Rd.	20	C3
Baillieswells Tce.	20	C4
Baird's Br.	21	H1
Baker Pl.	16	C1
Baker St.	16	C1
Balfron Pl.	15	E1
Balgownie Br.	8	C4
Balgownie Cres.	9	F4
Balgownie Ct.	13	E1
Balgownie Dr.	8	C4
Balgownie Gdns.	8	D4
Balgownie Pl.	8	B4
Balgownie Rd.	9	E4
Balgownie Way.	8	C4
Balloch Way.	3	E2
Balmoral Pk.	24	A5
Balmoral Pl.	16	B4
Balmoral Rd.	16	B4
Balmoral Tce.	16	B4
Balmoral Tce.	25	G5
Balnagask Circ.	17	H4
Balnagask Pl.	17	G4
Balnagask Rd.	17	F5
Balnagask Wk.	17	F4
Baltic St.	17	E1
Bank St.	12	A1
Bank St.	16	D4
Bankhead Ave.	6	B3
Bankhead Rd.	6	C3
Bannerman Pl.	10	C1
Barbour Br.	8	C3
Barclayhill Pl.	27	H3
Barra Wk.	10	B5
Barringer La.	31	H3
Barron St.	12	B1
Barvas Wk.	10	A4
Bath St.	16	D2
Battock Pl.	17	F4
Baxter Ct.	17	H3
Baxter Pl.	17	H3
Baxter St.	17	G3
Bayview Ct	13	F2
Bayview Rd.	15	G2
Bayview Rd. S.	15	G3
Beach Boulevard.	13	F5
Beach Esplanade.	9	G5
Beachview Ct	13	E1
Beaconhill Rd.	20	A5
Beaconhill Rd.	19	H2
Beaconsfield Pl.	15	H2
Beattie Ave.	12	A3
Beattie Pl.	12	A3
Bede House Ct.	12	D1
Bedford Ave.	12	B2
Bedford Pl.	12	C3
Bedford Rd.	12	C3
Beech Rd.	11	F3
Beech Rd.	31	E4
Beech-Hill Gdns.	15	F5
Beechgrove Ave.	15	H1
Beechgrove Gdns.	15	H1
Beechgrove Pl.	15	H1
Beechgrove Tce.	15	H1
Beechwood Ave.	11	G4
Beechwood Cl.	30	D4
Beechwood Ct.	11	F4
Beechwood Gdns.	30	D4
Beechwood Pl.	11	G3
Beechwood Pl.	30	D4
Beechwood Rd.	11	G3
Beechwood Wk.	11	G3
Belgrave Tce.	16	B1
Bellenden Wk.	19	F3
Bellfield Rd.	10	C4
Bellfield Rd.	9	F3
Bellmuir Gdns.	3	E2
Belmont Gdns.	12	B3
Belmont Rd.	12	B3
Belmont St.	16	D1
Belrorie Circ.	3	E2
Belvidere Cres.	16	A1
Belvidere La.	21	F3
Belvidere Rd.	21	E3
Belvidere St.	12	A5
Benbecula Rd.	10	A5
Berneray Pl.	10	B5
Berry St.	12	D5
Berryden Rd.	12	B4
Berryhill Pl.	28	C5
Berrymoss Ct.	3	F2
Berrymuir Pl	26	A3
Berrymuir Rd.	26	B3
Berrymuir Wynd.	26	A2
Berrywell Gdns.	3	E2
Berrywell Pl.	3	E2
Berrywell Rd.	3	E2
Berrywell Wk.	3	E2
Bervie Br.ow	24	B5
Bethany Gdns.	16	C3
Bethlin Mews.	29	F2
Bettridge Rd.	28	D4
Bieldside S. Rd.	20	D4
Binghill Cres.	19	G2
Binghill Dr.	19	F2
Binghill Hedge.	19	G1
Binghill Pk.	19	G2
Binghill Rd	19	G1
Binghill Rd. N.	19	G1
Binghill Rd. w.	19	G2
Birch Ave.	30	D4
Birch Rd.	11	G3
Birchfield Pl.	25	F5
Birkhall Parade.	11	E3
Birkhall Pl.	10	D3
Bishopsloch Row.	3	E3
Blackburn Pl.	12	D2
Blackfriars St.	16	C1
Blackhills Ct	30	C4
Blackhills Way.	30	C4
Blackhills Pl.	30	C3
Blackness Ave.	24	B5
Blackness Rd.	24	G4
Blacks La	17	F2
Blackthorn Cres.	11	G3
Blaikies Quay.	17	F2
Bleachfield Rd.	8	C2
Blenheim La.	16	A1
Blenheim Pl.	16	A1
Bloomfield Pl.	16	B4
Bloomfield Rd.	16	B4
Boa Vista	12	D3
Bodachra Pl.	8	C3
Bodachra Rd.	8	C3
Boddie Pl.	13	E4
Bon Accord Cres.	16	C2
Bon Accord Cres. La.	16	C2
Bon Accord La.	16	C2
Bon Accord Sq. E.	16	C2
Bon Accord Sq. W.	16	C2
Bon Accord St.	16	C3
Bon Accord Tce.	16	C2
Bonnymuir Pl.	11	H5
Bonnyview Dr.	10	C1
Bonnyview Pl.	10	C1
Bonnyview Rd.	10	C1
Booth Pl.	6	C5
Borrowstone Pl.	10	C5
Boswell Ave	26	D1
Boswell Rd	26	D1
Boswell Way	26	D1
Boswell Wk	26	D1
Boswell Wynd	26	D1
Bourtree Ave.	26	B3
Boyd Orr Ave.	23	F5
Boyd Orr Cl.	23	F4

Street	Page	Grid
Boyd Orr Pl.	23	F5
Boyd Orr Wk.	23	F5
Bracken Rd.	27	E3
Braecroft Ave.	31	F3
Braecroft Cres.	31	F2
Braecroft Dr.	31	F2
Braefoot Rd.	11	H4
Braehead Tce.	19	G2
Braehead Way.	8	D2
Braehead.	9	E3
Braemar Pl.	16	A4
Braeside Ave.	22	B1
Braeside Pl.	15	F5
Braeside Tce.	22	B1
Bramble Br.	11	F2
Brander Pl.	8	B3
Brebner Cres.	10	C2
Brebner Tce.	10	C2
Brent Rd.	2	B4
Bressay Br.	10	B4
Bridge of Dee.	23	E1
Bridge of Don.	9	F5
Bridge Pl.	16	D2
Bridge St.	16	D2
Brierfield Rd.	11	G3
Brierfield Tce.	11	G3
Bright St.	16	C4
Brighton Mews	18	B4
Brighton Pl.	16	A3
Brighton Pl.	18	B5
Brimmond View.	6	B1
Brimmond Cres.	31	E4
Brimmond Ct.	17	H4
Brimmond Ct.	31	E5
Brimmond Dr.	31	E5
Brimmond La.	30	D5
Brimmond Pl.	17	E5
Brimmond Pl.	31	E5
Brimmond Way	30	D5
Brimmond Wk.	30	D4
Brimmondside.	6	A5
Broad St.	16	D1
Broaddykes Ave.	29	F3
Broaddykes Cl.	29	F3
Broaddykes Cres.	29	F4
Broaddykes Dr.	29	F4
Broaddykes Pl.	29	F4
Broaddykes View.	29	F4
Broadfold Dr.	9	F3
Broadfold Rd.	9	F2
Broadfold Tce.	9	F3
Broadlands Gdns.	30	B3
Broadstraik Ave.	30	B4
Broadstraik Pl.	30	B4
Brodiach Ct.	31	G3
Brodinch Pl.	10	C4
Brodinch Rd.	10	C4
Brooke Cres.	9	E1
Broom Pk.	21	E2
Broomfield Pk.	26	C2
Broomfield Rd.	26	C2
Broomhill Ave.	16	A5
Broomhill Pl.	16	A5
Broomhill Rd.	16	A5
Broomhill Tce.	16	A5
Brough Pl	12	A3
Brown St.	12	A1
Bruce Hse.	14	B2
Bruce Wk.	24	A4
Brucklay Ct.	3	F3
Brunswick Pl.	16	C4
Bruntland Ct.	26	E4
Bruntland Pl.	27	E4
Bruntland Rd.	26	D3
Buchan Pl.	17	H4
Buchan Rd.	17	H4
Buchan Rd.	2	B3
Buchan Tce.	17	H4
Buchanan Gdns.	23	G3
Buchanan Pl.	23	G3
Buchanan Rd.	23	G3
Buckie Ave.	8	A2
Buckie Cl.	8	A2
Buckie Cres.	8	A2
Buckie Grv.	8	B2
Buckie Rd.	8	B2
Buckie Wk.	8	A2
Buckie Wynd.	8	B2
Bucklerburn Cl.	18	A3
Bucklerburn Dr.	18	B3
Bucklerburn Pk.	18	B3
Bucklerburn Pl.	18	B3
Bucklerburn Rd.	18	A3
Bucklerburn Vw.	18	B3
Bucklerburn Wynd.	18	A3
Bunstane Tce.	25	G5
Bunzeach Pl.	3	F2
Burnbank Pl.	17	G4
Burnbank Tce.	17	G4
Burnbrae Ave.	10	D5
Burnbrae Cres.	10	D5
Burnbrae Pl.	10	D5
Burnbutts Cres.	25	G5
Burndale Rd.	6	C3
Burnett Pl.	12	B2
Burnieboozle Cres.	14	D4
Burnieboozle Pl.	14	D4
Burns Gdns.	15	H3
Burns Gdns.	15	H3
Burns Rd.	15	H3
Burnside Dr.	3	F4
Burnside Dr.	9	F3
Burnside Gdns.	11	H5
Burnside Gdns.	27	F3
Burnside Rd	18	A5
Burnside Rd.	3	F4
Bute Way.	10	B5
Bydand Pl.	9	F1
Byron Ave.	10	D1
Byron Cres.	10	D1
Byron Pk.	10	D2
Byron Sq.	10	D1
Byron Tce.	10	C2
Cable's La.	17	E3
Cadenhead Pl.	12	A3
Cadenhead Rd.	12	A3
Caiesdykes Cres.	23	G3
Caiesdykes Dr.	23	G3
Caiesdykes Rd.	23	G3
Cairn Cres.	20	D3
Cairn Gdns.	20	D3
Cairn Pk.	20	D3
Cairn Rd.	20	D3
Cairn Rd.	18	C4
Cairn Side.	20	D3
Cairn Wk.	20	D3
Cairnaqueen Gdns.	15	G1
Cairnaqueen Pl.	15	G1
Cairncry Ave.	11	H3
Cairncry Cres.	11	H3
Cairncry Ct.	11	G3
Cairncry Rd.	11	H3
Cairncry Tce.	11	H3
Cairnfield Dr.	11	H5
Cairnfield Pl.	11	H5
Cairnfold Rd.	9	E3
Cairngorm Cres.	23	D2
Cairngorm Dr.	23	G3
Cairngorm Gdns.	23	D2
Cairngorm Pl.	23	G3
Cairngorm Rd.	23	F2
Cairngrassie Circ.	26	B3
Cairngrassie Dr.	26	B3
Cairnhill Rd.	28	B5
Cairnhillock Pl.	6	A5
Cairnie Dr.	12	A3
Cairnie Vw.	30	D2
Cairnlee Ave. E.	20	D3
Cairnlee Cres. N.	20	D3
Cairnlee Cres. S.	20	D3
Cairnlee Pk.	20	C3
Cairnlee Rd.	20	C3
Cairnlee Tce.	20	C3
Cairnton Ct.	31	F3
Cairnvale Cres.	23	G3
Cairnvale Tce.	23	G2
Cairnview Cres.	11	G3
Cairnwell Ave.	10	D3
Cairnwell Dr.	10	D3
Cairnwell Dr.	26	D2
Cairnwell Pl.	10	D3
Cairnwell Tce.	23	G3
Caledonian La.	16	D3
Caledonian Pl.	16	C3
Callum Park.	29	F2
Callum Path.	29	E2
Callum Wynd.	29	E2
Calsayseat Rd.	12	B4
Cameron Ave.	9	E2
Cameron Dr.	9	E2
Cameron Pl.	9	E3
Cameron Rd.	9	E3
Cameron St.	9	E3
Cameron Tce.	9	E3
Cameron Way.	9	E2
Cammach Circ.	26	B3
Camperdown Rd.	11	H5
Campsie Pl.	15	E1
Campus One.	8	C3
Campus Three.	8	D4
Campus Two.	8	D4
Canal Pl.	12	D4
Canal Rd.	12	C4
Canal St.	12	A1
Canal St.	12	D4
Caperstown Cres.	11	E2
Carden Pl.	16	A2
Carden Tce.	16	B2
Carden's Knowe	9	E3
Carlin Tce.	3	E3
Carlton Pl.	15	H1
Carmelite La.	16	D1
Carmelite St.	16	D1
Carnegie Cres.	15	F2
Carnegie Gdns.	15	F2
Carnie Dr.	12	A3
Carnoustie Cres.	8	C2
Carnoustie Gdns.	8	C2
Caroline Pl.	12	C5
Carron Pl.	10	D3
Cassie Cl.	25	F4
Castle Gate.	17	E1
Castle St.	17	E1
Castle Tce.	17	F1
Castlehill.	17	E1
Castleton Cres.	11	F4
Castleton Ct.	11	F4
Castleton Dr.	11	F4
Castleton La.	11	F4
Castleton Pk.	11	F4
Castleton Way.	11	F4
Catherine St.	12	C5
Catto Cres.	25	F4
Catto Wk.	25	F4
Cattofield Gdns.	12	A3
Cattofield Pl.	12	A3
Cattofield Tce.	12	A3
Causewayend.	12	D4
Cava Cl.	10	B5
Cedar Ct.	12	B3
Cedar Pl.	12	B4
Centre Point.	9	E1
Chapel Croft.	17	E1
Chapel Rd.	28	D4
Chapel St.	16	C1
Chapel St Mews	16	C2
Charles St.	12	C4
Charleston Cres	25	F5
Charleston Way.	25	F5
Charlestown Circ.	25	E5
Charlestown Rd.	25	E5
Charlotte Gdns.	12	C5
Charlotte Pl.	12	C5
Charlotte St.	12	C5
Chattan Pl.	16	A3
Cherry Rd.	11	G3
Chestnut Row.	12	B4
Cheyne Rd.	12	D1
Church St.	11	H1
Church St.	17	F1
Church Wk.	12	D2
Churchill Rd.	9	F3
Claremont Gdns.	16	B3
Claremont Gro.	16	A3
Claremont Pl.	16	A3
Claremont St.	16	A3
Clarence St.	17	F1
Clarke St.	11	F1
Clarks La.	12	D1
Clashbog Pl.	6	A5
Clasherknowe.	9	E3
Clashfarquhar Cres.	26	D2
Clashnettie Pl.	3	F3
Clashrodney Ave.	25	E5
Clashrodney Rd.	25	E5
Clashrodney Way.	25	E5
Clashrodney Wk.	25	E5
Claymore Ave.	9	G1
Claymore Ave.	27	G3
Claymore Dr.	9	G2
Clerk Maxwell Cres.	23	F4
Cliff Pk.	21	G2
Cliff Pl.	17	G4
Cliff View.	28	B5
Clifton La.	8	B5
Clifton Pl.	8	B5
Clifton Rd.	8	B5
Cloghill Pl.	10	C5
Clova Cres.	29	E3
Clova Pk.	29	F3
Clover Meadow	30	B3
Cloverfield Ct.	6	A4
Cloverfield Gdns.	6	B4
Cloverfield Pl.	6	A4
Cloverhill Cres.	8	D3
Cloverhill Gdns.	8	C4
Cloverhill Rd.	9	F2
Clunie Pl.	10	D3
Clyde St.	17	E1
Coldstone Ave.	29	E3
Coll Wk.	10	B5
College Bounds.	12	D3
College St.	16	D2
Colleston Ave.	8	D1
Colleston Circ.	8	D1
Colleston Cres.	8	D1
Colleston Dr.	8	D1
Colleston Path	8	D1
Colleston Pl.	8	D1
Colleston Rd.	8	D2
Colleston St.	8	D1
Colleston Way.	8	D1
Colonsay Cres.	10	B5
Colsea Rd.	25	G5
Colsea Tce.	25	G5
Colthill Circ.	19	F2
Colthill Cres.	19	F1
Colthill Dr.	19	F2

Colthill Rd. 19 F2
Colville Pl. 13 E4
Commerce Lane . . 17 F1
Commerce St. 17 E1
Commercial Quay.. . 17 F2
Conningham Gdns.. 12 B1
Conningham Rd.... 12 C1
Conningham Tce. . . 12 C1
Constitution Ct.. . . 13 E5
Constitution La. . . . 13 F5
Constitution St.. . . . 13 F5
Contlaw Br. 19 G2
Contlaw Pl. 19 G2
Contlaw Rd. 19 F2
Cookston Rd. 27 F3
Corby Tce. 3 E2
Cordyce Vw. 2 D3
Cormorant Br. 25 E4
Corndavon Tce.. . . 11 E4
Cornhill Ct. 11 G3
Cornhill Dr. 11 G3
Cornhill Gdns.. . . . 11 G3
Cornhill Rd. 11 H4
Cornhill Sq. 11 H3
Cornhill Tce. 11 H3
Cornhill Way. 11 G4
Cornyhaugh Rd. . . . 18 A3
Coronation Ct.. . . . 18 C4
Coronation Rd. . . . 18 C4
Correction Wynd. . . 16 D1
Corrennie Circ. 3 E1
Corse Ave 29 F1
Corse Gdns. 29 F1
Corse Wynd 29 F1
Corthan Cres. 23 D2
Corthan Dr. 23 D2
Corthan Pl. 23 D2
Corunna Rd. 9 G3
Cothal Vw. 2 D1
Cottage Br. 16 B3
Cotton St. 13 F5
Coull Gdns. 9 E4
Coull Gdns. 29 E3
Coull Green 29 E2
Countesswells Ave. 14 D4
Countesswells Cres. 14 D5
Countesswells Pl. . . 14 D4
Countesswells Rd. . 14 D5
Countesswells Tce. . 14 D4
Cove Circ. 25 F5
Cove Cres.. . . . . . . 25 F5
Cove Crt. 25 F5
Cove Gdns 25 F5
Cove Path.. . . . . . . 25 G5
Cove Pl. 25 F5
Cove Rd.. . . . . 25 F5
Cove Way 25 F5
Cove Wk. 25 F5
Cove Wynd. 25 F5
Covenanters Dr. . . 23 G1
Covenanters Row.. 23 F1
Cowan Pl. 12 B1
Craibstone Ave. . . 6 B1
Craibstone La.. . . . 16 C2
Craig Gdns. 20 D3
Craig Pl.. . . . . 17 E4
Craig Pl.. . . . . 28 D4
Craigend Ave. 26 D2
Craigendarroch Ave.11 E3
Craigendarroch Pl. . 11 E3
Craigharr Gables.. 6 C2
Craighill Tce.. . . . . 25 G5
Craigie Loanings.. 16 A1
Craigie Pk. 16 A1
Craigie Pk. Pl. 16 A1
Craigie St. 12 C5
Craigiebuckler Ave. 14 D3

Craigiebuckler Dr... 14 D3
Craigiebuckler Pl. . . 14 D3
Craigiebuckler Tce.. 15 E3
Craigieburn Pk. 15 E4
Craigielea Ave. 15 G5
Craigielea Gdns.. . . 15 G5
Craigievar Cres. . . . 22 D2
Craigievar Pl.. . . . . . 22 D1
Craigievar Rd. 22 D2
Craigievar Tce. 22 D2
Craigmaroinn Gdns. 24 D3
Craignook Rd. 3 E2
Craigpark. 24 A2
Craigshaw Cres. . . . 24 A1
Craigshaw Dr. 23 D1
Craigshaw Pl. 23 D1
Craigshaw Rd.. . . . . 24 A1
Craigshaw St. 24 A2
Craigston Gdns. . . . 31 G2
Craigston Pl. 31 G2
Craigston Rd. 31 G2
Craigton Ave. 15 F5
Craigton Cres. 18 B4
Craigton Ct. 15 G5
Craigton Dr. 18 B4
Craigton Grv 18 B4
Craigton Pk. 15 F5
Craigton Rd. 21 G1
Craigton Tce. 15 F5
Craigton Tce. 18 B4
Cranford Pl. 15 H5
Cranford Rd. 15 H5
Cranford Tce. 15 H5
Cranhill Br. 28 D4
Cranhill Pl.. . . . . 28 D4
Crathie Gdns. 16 B5
Crathie Tce. 16 B5
Crawpeel Rd. 24 B4
Crawton Ness.. . . . . 24 B5
Creel Ave. 25 F5
Creel Crt. 25 E5
Creel Rd.. . . . . 25 F5
Creel Wynd 25 F5
Crimon Pl. 16 C1
Croft Pl.. . . . . 10 D4
Croft Rd. 10 D4
Croft Ter. 10 D4
Crollshillock Pl.. . . 28 B5
Cromar Gdns. 29 F2
Crombie Acres 30 B3
Crombie Circ. 30 B3
Crombie Cl.. . . . . . . 30 C3
Crombie Dr. 30 B3
Crombie Pl. 17 F4
Crombie Pl. 30 B3
Crombie Rd. 30 B3
Crombie Wynd 30 B3
Cromwell Ct. 15 H3
Cromwell Gdns. . . . 15 G3
Cromwell Rd.. . . . . 15 G3
Crooked La. 16 D1
Crookfold Gdns. . . . 9 F3
Crookfold Pl.. . . . . 9 F3
Crossgates. 6 C3
Crown Cres. 18 C3
Crown La. 16 D2
Crown Pl. 18 C4
Crown St. 16 D2
Crown Tce 18 C4
Crown Tce. 16 D2
Cruden Cres. 10 C2
Cruden Pk. 10 C2
Cruden Pl. 10 C2
Cruickshank Cres. . 6 B5
Cruickshank Ct. . . 30 B5
Cruickshanks Cres. 23 F3
Culter Den. 18 A5

Culter House Rd.... 19 E3
Cults Ave. 21 E2
Cults Ct. 21 F3
Cults Gdns.. . . . . . . 21 F3
Cummings Pk. Circ. 11 F2
Cummings Pk. Cres. 11 E2
Cummings Pk. Dr.. 11 F2
Cummings Pk. Rd. . 11 E2
Cummings Pk. Tce. 11 E2
Cuparstone Ct.. . . . 16 B3
Cuparstone Row. . . 16 B3
Cypress Ave. 4 D1
Cypress Grove. 5 E1
Cypress Walk.. . . . . 4 D1
Dalmaik Cres. 18 B4
Dalmaik Tce. 18 B3
Dalmuinzie Rd. . . . 20 B4
Dancing Cairns Cres. 10 D1
Dancing Cairns Pl. . 7 E5
Danestone Circ. . . . 11 F1
Danestone Cres.. . . 9 E3
Danestone Pl. 9 E3
Darroch Pk. 21 E3
Davan Pk. 8 D4
Davidson Dr.. . . . . . 10 C2
Davidson Gdns. . . . 10 C2
Davidson Pl. 10 C2
Dean Gdns. 31 G3
Deansloch Cres. . . . 10 D2
Deansloch Pl. 10 D2
Deansloch Tce. 10 D2
Dee Ct.. . . . . 16 C2
Dee Pl.. . . . . 16 C2
Dee St. 16 C2
Deemount Ave. . . . 16 D4
Deemount Gdns. . . 16 D4
Deemount Rd.. . . . 16 D4
Deemount Tce. . . . 16 D4
Deer Rd. 8 A5
Deeside Ave. 22 C1
Deeside Cres. 22 B1
Deeside Dr. 22 C1
Deeside Gdns. 22 B1
Deeside Pk. 22 C1
Deeside Pl. 22 C1
Deeside Tce. 22 C1
Deevale Cres. 23 F2
Deevale Gdns. 23 G2
Deevale Rd. 23 F2
Deevale Tce. 23 F2
Deeview Rd S. 21 F3
Delgaty La. 3 E2
Dempsey Tce. 12 C1
Denburn Ct. 16 C1
Denburn Rd.. . . . . 16 D1
Denmore Gdns.. . . 9 E4
Denmore Pl 5 F2
Denmore Rd.. . . . . 9 F1
Denseat Ct. 14 B1
Derbeth Cres. 10 C5
Derbeth Park 29 G1
Derry Ave. 11 E4
Derry Pl.. . . . . 11 E4
Desswood Pl. 15 H2
Devanha Cres.. . . . 16 D3
Devanha Gdns E. . 16 D4
Devanha Gdns S. . 16 D4
Devanha Gdns W. . 16 D4
Devanha La. 16 D3
Devanha Tce. 16 D3
Devenick Dr. 27 F3
Devenick Pl. 22 C2
Deveron Rd. 10 D3
Devonshire Rd.. . . 15 H3
Diamond La. 16 C1
Diamond Pl. 16 C1
Diamond St. 16 C1

Dickson Tce. 10 C3
Dill Pl. 8 B5
Dill Rd.. . . . . 8 C5
Dinbaith Pl. 10 C5
Dominies Ct. 11 G2
Dominies Rd.. . . . . 11 G2
Don Ct. 8 A5
Don Gdns. 8 B5
Don Pl. 12 A1
Don Pl.. . . . . 3 E3
Don St. 8 B5
Don St. 9 E4
Don Tce. 8 B5
Donald Pl. 12 B5
Donbank Pl.. . . . . . 8 B5
Donbank Tce. 8 B5
Donmouth Cres. . . 9 G4
Donmouth Ct. 9 F4
Donmouth Gdns... 9 G4
Donmouth Rd.. . . . 9 G4
Donmouth Tce. . . . 9 F4
Donside Ct. 8 C5
Donview Hse. 13 E1
Donview Pl. 8 B5
Donview Rd. 8 B5
Doolie Ness. 24 B5
Douglas La. 12 D2
Douglas Pl. 12 D2
Downies Br.. . . . . . 17 F5
Downies Pl.. . . . . . 17 G4
Downies Rd.. . . . . 27 C5
Drinnes Cres. 3 E2
Drumthwacket Dr... 26 A3
Dubford Ave. 5 E2
Dubford Cres. 5 E2
Dubford Gdns. . . . 5 E1
Dubford Grv. 4 D1
Dubford Pk. 8 D1
Dubford Pl. 5 E2
Dubford Rd.. . . . . 5 E2
Dubford Rise. 4 D1
Dubford Tce. 4 D2
Dubford Wk. 4 D1
Duff St. 13 E5
Dugald Baird Ct. . . 23 F4
Dugald Baird Sq... 23 F4
Dulnain Rd. 10 C4
Dumgoyne Pl. 15 E1
Dunbar St. 12 D1
Dunbennan Rd.. . . 3 F2
Dunecht Gdns. . . . 30 C3
Dunecht Rd. 30 C3
Dunlin Cres. 25 E4
Dunlin Ct 28 C3
Dunlin Rd. 2 B3
Dunlin Rd. 25 E4
Dunmail Ave. 21 F3
Dunvegan Ave. . . . 27 E3
Dunvegan Cres. . . 27 E3
Dunvegan Pl.. . . . . 27 E3
Duthie Pl. 15 G5
Duthie Tce. 15 H5
Dyce Dr. 2 B5
Dykeside Br. 6 A5
Dykeside Way 6 B5
Earl's Court Gdns. . 15 G2
Earlspark Ave. . . . 20 C3
Earlspark Circ. . . . 20 C2
Earlspark Cres. . . . 20 C3
Earlspark Dr. 20 C3
Earlspark Gdns. . . 20 C3
Earlspark Rd. 20 C3
Earlspark Way. . . . 20 C3
Earlswells Dr. 20 D3
Earlswells Pl. 20 D3
Earlswells Rd. 20 D3
Earlswells Vw.. . . . 20 D3

Earlswells Wk..	20	D3
Earns Heugh Ave.	25	F5
Earns Heugh Circ.	25	F5
Earns Heugh Cres.	25	F5
Earns Heugh Pl.	25	F5
Earns Heugh Rd.	25	F5
Earns Heugh View.	25	F5
Earns Heugh Way.	25	F5
Earns Heugh Wk.	25	F5
East Craibstone St.	16	C2
East Dock St.	17	F2
East Green.	16	D1
East Main Ave.	11	E4
East North St.	13	E5
Easter Ct.	26	A3
Easter Dr.	26	A4
Easter Pl.	26	A4
Eastside Ave.	31	G3
Eastside Dr.	31	F2
Eastside Gdns.	6	A3
Eastside Green.	31	F2
Eastsyde Pl.	26	B4
Eday Cres.	14	D1
Eday Dr..	14	C1
Eday Rd.	14	D1
Eday Sq.	10	C5
Eden Pl.	16	B1
Eden Side.	18	A3
Edgehill Rd..	15	F1
Edgehill Tce.	15	F1
Edmond Gdns.	29	G5
Elder Pl.	12	A3
Ellerslie Rd..	6	C3
Ellon Rd.	9	F3
Elm Pl.	12	B4
Elmbank Rd.	12	C4
Elmbank Tce.	12	C4
Elmfield Ave.	12	C3
Elmfield Tce.	12	C3
Elphinstone Ct.	8	B5
Elphinstone Rd.	12	D2
Elrick Circ.	8	C3
Elsick Pl.	28	C4
Endrick Pl.	15	E1
Eriskay Dr.	10	B5
Errol Pl.	13	E4
Errol St.	13	E4
Erskine St.	12	C3
Esk Pl.	10	D3
Esplanade.	13	F5
Esslemont Ave.	16	B1
Exchange Lane	16	D1
Exchange St.	16	D1
Exchequer Row.	17	E1
Exhibition Ave.	9	G2
Exploration Dr.	9	G2
Fairies Knowe.	6	A5
Fairley Rd.	29	G4
Fairlie St.	11	F1
Fairview Ave.	7	H3
Fairview Br.	8	A3
Fairview Circ.	7	H3
Fairview Cres.	8	A3
Fairview Dr.	8	A3
Fairview Gdns.	7	H3
Fairview Gro.	7	H3
Fairview Manor Wk.	8	A3
Fairview Parade.	7	H3
Fairview Pk.	7	H3
Fairview Pl.	7	H3
Fairview Rd.	7	H2
Fairview St.	8	A3
Fairview Tce.	7	H3
Fairview Way.	7	H3
Fairview Wk.	8	A3
Fairview Wynd.	8	A3
Falkland Ave.	25	G4
Fallow Rd.	30	B3
Fara Cl.	10	B5
Farburn Tce.	2	D4
Fare Pk. Circ.	31	E2
Fare Pk. Cres.	31	E2
Fare Pk. Dr.	31	E2
Fare Pk. Gdns.	31	E2
Farmers Hall.	12	C5
Farquhar Ave.	17	G4
Farquhar Br.	17	F4
Farquhar La.	17	F4
Farquhar Rd.	17	F5
Fassiefern. Ave.	9	E1
Faulds Cres.	23	G1
Faulds Gate	23	G2
Faulds Row.	23	G2
Faulds Wynd.	23	G2
Fergidon Ct.	6	D4
Fergus Pl.	3	E2
Fern Dr.	26	D3
Fern Pl.	26	D3
Fernhill Dr.	10	D4
Fernhill Pl.	10	D5
Fernhill Rd.	10	C5
Fernie Br.	24	A3
Fernielea Cres.	14	D1
Fernielea Pl.	14	D1
Fernielea Rd.	14	D1
Ferrier Cres.	12	B1
Ferrier Gdns.	12	A1
Ferry Pl.	17	F2
Ferryhill Dr.	10	D5
Ferryhill Pl.	16	C3
Ferryhill Rd.	16	C3
Ferryhill Tce.	16	D3
Fetach Wk.	3	E2
Fifehill Pk.	3	F3
Findhorn Pl.	10	C4
Findon Ness.	24	G5
Finnan Br.	17	H4
Finnan Pl.	17	G4
Fintray Rd.	14	D3
Firhill Pl.	12	D3
Fish St.	17	F1
Fittick Pl.	25	F4
Flourmill La.	16	D1
Flowershill Gdns.	8	D3
Fonthill Rd.	16	D3
Fonthill Tce.	16	C4
Forbes St.	12	C5
Forbesfield La.	15	H4
Forbesfield Rd.	15	H4
Forehill La.	9	E3
Forest Ave.	15	H3
Forest Ave. La.	15	H3
Forest Rd.	15	H2
Foresterhill Ct.	11	H5
Foresters Ave.	6	C1
Formartine Rd.	12	B1
Forresterhill Ct.	11	H5
Forresterhill Rd.	11	F3
Forrit Br.	6	A3
Forties Rd..	2	B4
Forvie Ave.	8	D2
Forvie Circ.	8	C1
Forvie Cl.	8	C1
Forvie Cres.	8	C1
Forvie La.	8	C2
Forvie Path.	8	C2
Forvie Pl.	8	C1
Forvie Rd.	8	C1
Forvie St.	8	C1
Forvie Tce.	8	C2
Forvie Way.	8	C2
Fountain Grange.	12	A1
Fountainhall Rd.	15	H1
Fountville Ct.	12	A1
Foveran Path.	8	C1
Foveran Rise.	8	C1
Foveran St.	8	C1
Foveran Way.	8	C1
Fowler Ave.	11	F1
Fowlershill Gdns.	8	D1
Fraser Ct.	12	C4
Fraser Dr.	30	C4
Fraser Pl.	12	C4
Fraser Rd.	12	C4
Fraser St.	12	C4
Fraserfield Gdns.	9	E3
Frederick St.	13	E5
Friarsfield Rd.	21	F2
Friendship Tce.	16	A3
Froghall Ave.	12	C3
Froghall Gdns.	12	C4
Froghall Pl.	12	C3
Froghall Rd.	12	D4
Froghall Tce.	12	C4
Froghall View.	12	D3
Fullerton Ct.	7	H5
Fulmar Ct.	28	C3
Gadie Cres.	10	D3
Gaelic La.	16	D1
Gairn Circ.	16	B4
Gairn Cres.	16	B4
Gairn Ct.	16	B5
Gairn Rd.	16	B4
Gairn Tce.	16	B4
Gairnshiel Ave.	11	E3
Gairnshiel Pl..	11	E3
Gairsay Dr.	10	D5
Gairsay Rd.	10	D5
Gairsay Sq.	10	C5
Gaitside Dr.	22	C2
Gaitside Pl.	22	C2
Gaitside Rd.	22	C2
Gaitside Tce.	22	B2
Gallowgate.	12	D5
Gallowhill Tce.	3	F2
Garden Rd.	21	E2
Gardner Cres.	23	F3
Gardner Dr.	23	F4
Gardner Pl.	23	F3
Gardner Rd.	23	F3
Gardner Wk.	23	F3
Garmaddie La.	3	E2
Garthdee Cres.	22	D1
Garthdee Dr.	22	D1
Garthdee Gdns.	22	D1
Garthdee Rd.	22	B2
Garthdee Tce.	22	D1
Garvock Wynd	17	E1
Gateside Cres.	22	C2
George St.	12	C5
Gerrard St.	12	D5
Gilbert Rd.	6	C4
Gilcomston Pk.	16	C1
Gilcomstoun Land.	16	C1
Gillahill Pl.	11	E4
Gillahill Rd.	11	E4
Gillespie Cres.	12	A3
Gillespie Pl.	12	A3
Girdleness Rd.	17	E5
Girdleness Tce.	17	E5
Girdlestone Pl.	17	G4
Gladstone Pl.	15	H3
Gladstone Pl..	3	E3
Gladstone Pl.	8	B5
Glascairn Ave.	27	E3
Glascairn Pl.	27	E3
Glashieburn.	8	D1
Glashieburn Way.	9	E3
Glashieburn Wk.	9	E3
Glebe Ct.	27	F3
Glen Ave.	3	E3
Glen Dr.	3	E3
Glen Gdns.	3	E3
Glen Grv	16	B2
Glen Rd.	3	E3
Glenbervie Rd.	17	F4
Glendee Tce.	21	G2
Gleneagles Ave.	8	C2
Gleneagles Dr..	8	C2
Gleneagles Gdns.	8	C2
Gleneagles Wk.	8	C2
Glenfern Rd.	10	D4
Glenhome Ave.	3	E3
Glenhome Cres.	3	E3
Glenhome Ct.	3	E3
Glenhome Gdns..	3	E4
Glenhome Tce.	3	E4
Glenhome Wk.	3	F3
Glentanar Cres.	3	F2
Golden Sq.	16	C1
Golf Rd.	13	F2
Golf Rd.	20	D4
Golfview Rd.	20	D4
Goodhope Rd.	7	E4
Gordon Ave.	9	E3
Gordon Cl.	31	E3
Gordon Ct.	9	E1
Gordon Gdns	31	E3
Gordon Lane	15	G5
Gordon Lennox Cres.	9	E1
Gordon Mills Cres.	8	B5
Gordon Mills Pl.	8	C5
Gordon Mills Rd.	8	B5
Gordon Pl.	9	E3
Gordon Rd.	15	G5
Gordon Rd.	15	G5
Gordon Rd.	9	E3
Gordon St.	16	C2
Gordon Tce.	15	G5
Gordon Tce.	3	E3
Gordondale Ct.	15	H1
Gordondale Rd..	15	H1
Gorse Circ.	26	A3
Gorsehill Gdns..	8	D3
Gort Rd..	8	C5
Goval Tce.	3	E3
Gowanbrae Rd.	20	C4
Graeme Ave.	3	E2
Grampian Gdns.	3	F4
Grampian La.	17	E4
Grampian Pl.	17	E4
Grampian Rd.	17	E4
Grampion Ct.	17	H4
Grandholm St.	12	A1
Granitehill Hse.	11	E1
Granitehill Pl.	11	F3
Granitehill Rd.	11	E1
Grant Cl.	31	E4
Grant's Pl.	12	D2
Granton Pl.	16	A3
Granville Pl.	15	H4
Gray Ct.	14	D1
Gray St.	16	B5
Great Northern Rd.	8	A5
Great Southern Rd.	16	B4
Great Southern Rd.	23	F1
Great Western Pl.	16	B3
Great Western Rd.	16	A4
Green Wk.	11	G3
Greenbank Cres.	24	B1
Greenbank Pl.	24	B1
Greenbank Rd.	24	B1
Greenbrae Ave.	9	F1
Greenbrae Circ.	5	E2
Greenbrae Cres.	5	E2
Greenbrae Dr.	5	E2
Greenbrae Gdns. N.	5	E2
Greenbrae Gdns. S.	5	E2

Greenbrae Wk.	5	E2
Greenburn Dr.	6	B2
Greenburn Dr.	6	B4
Greenburn Rd.	6	A2
Greenburn Rd. N.	6	A2
Greenburn Tce.	6	B4
Greenfern Ave.	10	C4
Greenfern Rd.	10	D4
Greenhole Pl.	9	E2
Greenmore Gdns.	12	A2
Greenwell Pl.	17	G5
Greenwell Rd.	17	G5
Gregness Gdns.	17	F5
Greig Ct.	12	C5
Greyhope Rd.	17	G3
Greystone Pl.	28	C4
Groats Rd.	14	B2
Grosvenor Pl.	16	B1
Grosvenor Tce.	16	B1
Grove Cres.	11	H4
Guestrow.	16	D1
Guild St.	16	D2
Gullymoss Gdns.	31	F2
Gullymoss Pl.	31	F2
Gullymoss Vw.	31	F1
Hallfield Cres.	10	C5
Hallfield Rd.	10	C5
Hamilton Pl.	15	H1
Hammerfield Ave.	15	H5
Hammersmith Rd.	15	H4
Hanover St.	17	F1
Harcourt Rd.	11	G5
Hardgate Gdns.	16	D4
Hardgate La.	16	B4
Hardgate.	16	B3
Harehill Rd.	8	D3
Hareness Circ.	24	B4
Hareness Pk.	24	G4
Hareness Rd.	24	B3
Harlaw Pl.	15	G3
Harlaw Rd.	15	G3
Harlaw Tce.	15	G3
Harriet St.	16	D1
Harris Dr.	12	B1
Harris Tce.	12	C1
Harrow Rd.	12	D1
Harthill Pl.	13	E4
Hartington Rd.	16	A3
Harvesthill.	31	B3
Hasman Tce.	25	G5
Hawthorn Cres.	11	E3
Hawthorn Tce.	13	F5
Hay's Way	30	C3
Hayfield Cres.	11	H3
Hayfield Pl.	11	H3
Hayton Rd.	8	C5
Hazel Dr.	30	D4
Hazledene Rd.	14	D3
Hazlehead Ave.	14	D2
Hazlehead Cres.	14	C2
Hazlehead Gdns.	14	C2
Hazlehead Pl.	14	C2
Hazlehead Rd.	14	C2
Hazlehead Tce.	14	C2
Headland Ct.	23	E1
Headland Ct.	28	D4
Heather Pl.	27	E4
Heathfield Pk.	28	B5
Heathryfold Circ.	10	D1
Heathryfold Dr.	10	D1
Heathryfold Pl.	10	D1
Henderson Dr.	30	D5
Hermitage Ave.	12	C2
Hetherwick Rd.	23	F3
High St.	12	D2
Highgate Gdns	23	D2
Hill Of Rubislaw.	15	F3
Hill Rd.	10	D4
Hill St.	12	C5
Hillcrest Pl.	11	F2
Hillhead Rd.	20	A4
Hillhead Rd.	28	D4
Hillhead Tce.	12	D3
Hillocks Way.	6	B5
Hillside Cres	18	B4
Hillside Cres.	31	F1
Hillside Gdns.	31	E2
Hillside Pl.	18	B4
Hillside Rd.	31	F2
Hillside Rd.	18	B4
Hillside Tce.	27	F4
Hillside Vw.	31	F2
Hillswick Rd.	10	A4
Hillswick Wk.	10	A4
Hilltop Ave.	21	E2
Hilltop Ave.	31	E1
Hilltop Cres.	31	E1
Hilltop Dr.	31	E1
Hilltop Gdns.	31	E1
Hilltop Rd.	21	E2
Hillview Ave.	31	F1
Hillview Cres.	20	D2
Hillview Dr.	21	E2
Hillview Rd.	21	E3
Hillview Rd.	24	B1
Hillview Rd.	31	F1
Hillview Rd.	18	B4
Hillview Tce.	21	E3
Hillylands Rd.	10	D5
Hilton Ave.	12	A2
Hilton Circ.	11	H3
Hilton Ct	11	G2
Hilton Dr.	11	H3
Hilton Pl.	12	A2
Hilton Rd.	12	A1
Hilton St.	12	A2
Hilton Tce.	12	A2
Hilton Wk.	11	H2
Holburn Pl.	16	B4
Holburn Rd.	16	B3
Holburn St.	16	B3
Holland Pl.	12	C4
Holland St.	12	C4
Hollybank Pl.	16	B3
Holmhead Pl.	6	B5
Homelea	30	B4
Hopecroft Ave.	6	A3
Hopecroft Dr.	6	A3
Hopecroft Gdns.	6	B3
Hopecroft Tce.	6	A3
Hopetoun Ave.	6	A4
Hopetoun Cres.	6	A4
Hopetoun Ct.	6	B3
Hopetoun Dr.	6	A4
Hopetoun Gra.	6	A3
Hopetoun Green.	6	A4
Hopetoun Rd.	6	A4
Hopetoun Tce.	6	A4
Hosefield Ave.	11	H5
Hosefield Rd.	11	H5
Howburn Pl.	16	B3
Howe Moss Ave.	2	A2
Howe Moss Dr.	2	A3
Howe Moss Pl.	2	A2
Howe Moss Rd.	2	A3
Howe Moss Tce.	2	A2
Howes Cres.	10	D1
Howes Dr.	10	D1
Howes Pl.	10	D1
Howes Rd.	6	C5
Howes Vw.	6	C5
Howie La.	18	C5
Hunter Pl.	13	E4
Huntly St.	16	C1
Hutcheon Ct.	12	C5
Hutcheon Gdns.	9	F4
Hutcheon Low Dr.	7	F5
Hutcheon Low Pl.	7	F4
Hutcheon St.	12	C5
Hutchison Tce.	15	G5
Hutton La.	10	D2
Hutton Pl.	10	D2
Hutton Rd.	2	B3
Huxterstone Ct.	29	F4
Huxterstone Drive.	29	F4
Huxterstone Pl.	29	F4
Huxterstone Tce.	29	F4
Imperial Pl.	16	D4
Inchbrae Dr.	22	C2
Inchbrae Rd.	22	C2
Inchbrae Tce.	22	B2
Inchgarth Rd.	21	H3
Ingram Wk.	24	A3
Intown Rd.	9	F2
Invercauld Gdns.	11	E3
Invercauld Pl.	11	E3
Invercauld Rd.	11	E3
Invergordon Ct.	9	F5
Inverurie Rd.	6	B4
Irvine Pl.	16	A4
Islay Pl.	10	C4
Ivanhoe Pl.	22	C1
Ivanhoe Rd.	22	B2
Ivanhoe Wk.	22	B2
Jacks Br.	16	B1
Jackson Tce.	13	E4
Jamaica St.	13	E4
James St.	17	E1
Jamieson Quay.	17	F2
Janesfield Manor.	22	B2
Jasmine Pl.	13	E5
Jasmine Tce.	13	E5
Jasmine Way.	13	E5
Jesmond Ave.	8	B2
Jesmond Ave. N.	8	B2
Jesmond Circ.	4	A1
Jesmond Dr.	4	B1
Jesmond Gdns.	4	A1
Jesmond Grv.	4	A1
Jesmond Rd.	8	C1
Jesmond Sq.	8	B2
John Arthur Ct.	29	H5
John Park Pl.	8	B3
John St.	12	C5
John St.	2	D4
Johnston Gdns. E.	18	A3
Johnston Gdns. N.	18	B3
Johnston Gdns. W.	18	A4
Jopp's La.	12	D5
Juniper Pl.	26	C2
Jura Pl.	10	B5
Justice Mill Br.	16	B2
Justice Mill La.	16	C2
Justice St.	17	E1
Jute St.	12	D4
Kaimhill Circ.	22	D1
Kaimhill Gdns.	22	D1
Kaimhill Rd.	22	D1
Keir Circ.	30	C3
Kemnay Pl.	15	E3
Kemp St.	11	F1
Kenfield Cres.	15	F4
Kenfield Pl.	15	G5
Kennerty Mill Rd.	18	B5
Kennerty Pk.	18	A5
Kennerty Rd.	18	A5
Kepplehills Dr.	6	A4
Kepplehills Rd.	6	B5
Kepplestone Ave.	15	F3
Kerloch Gdns.	14	C5
Kerloch Pl.	17	E5
Kettlehills Cres.	11	E2
Kettlehills La.	11	E2
Kettlehills Rd.	11	E2
Kettochs Mill Rd.	8	D4
Kettock Gdns.	8	C2
Kidd St.	16	C1
Kildrummy Rd.	14	D3
Kilsyth Rd.	23	D3
Kinaldie Cres.	14	D3
Kincorth Circ.	23	G2
Kincorth Cres.	23	G1
Kincorth Gdns.	23	G1
Kincorth Land	23	D2
Kincorth Pl.	23	G1
King George IV Br.	16	C5
King St.	12	D3
King St.	13	E4
King's Cres.	12	D4
King's Cross Ave.	15	F2
King's Cross Rd.	15	E2
King's Cross Tce.	15	E2
King's Cross.	15	F1
King's Ct.	8	B5
King's Gate	15	F1
King's Walk.	6	C4
Kingsford Rd.	10	C4
Kingshill Ave.	15	F1
Kingshill Rd.	15	F1
Kingshill Tce.	15	F1
Kingsland Pl.	12	C5
Kingsway.	6	C4
Kingswell Cres	29	G1
Kingswells Ave.	29	E2
Kingswells Dr.	29	E2
Kingswells View	30	D1
Kingswood Ave.	29	G3
Kingswood Cres.	29	G3
Kingswood Dr.	29	G3
Kingswood Gdns.	29	G4
Kingswood Grv.	29	G3
Kingswood Mews.	29	F3
Kingswood Path.	29	G3
Kingswood Rd.	29	G3
Kingswood Wlk.	29	G3
Kinkell Rd.	14	D3
Kinmundy Ave.	31	F3
Kinmundy Dr.	31	G3
Kinmundy Gdns.	31	G3
Kinmundy Green.	31	G3
Kinmundy Lodge	31	F2
Kinnaird Pl.	12	B1
Kinord Circ.	8	D4
Kintore Gdns.	12	C5
Kintore Pl.	12	B5
Kirk Brae.	21	E2
Kirk Cres N.	21	E2
Kirk Cres S.	21	F2
Kirk Dr.	21	F2
Kirk Pl.	21	E2
Kirk Tce.	21	E2
Kirkbrae Ave.	21	E2
Kirkbrae Ct.	21	F2
Kirkbrae Dr.	20	D2
Kirkbrae Mews.	21	F2
Kirkbrae Vw.	21	E2
Kirkhill Dr	2	B2
Kirkhill Pl.	17	F5
Kirkhill Pl.	2	B3
Kirkhill Rd.	17	F5
Kirkhill Rd.	2	B3
Kirkside Ct.	31	F3
Kirkton Ave.	2	D1
Kirkton Ave.	30	B3
Kirkton Gdns.	30	B3
Kirkton Pl.	30	B3
Kirkwall Ave.	10	A4
Kittybrewster Sq.	12	B3

Name	Pg	Grid
Laburnum Wk.	11	G3
Lade Cres.	6	B2
Ladywell Pl.	17	G5
Laird Gdns.	8	A2
Lamond Pl.	12	B4
Lang Stracht.	10	C5
Langdykes Cres.	25	F4
Langdykes Dr.	24	B5
Langdykes Rd.	25	F4
Langdykes Way.	24	B5
Langstane Pl.	16	C2
Larch Rd.	11	G3
Larg Dr	30	A3
Laurel Ave.	8	B3
Laurel Br.	8	A4
Laurel Dr.	8	A4
Laurel Gdns.	8	B3
Laurel Grv.	8	B3
Laurel Pl.	8	A4
Laurel Rd.	8	A4
Laurel Tce.	8	A4
Laurel View.	8	A4
Laurel Wynd.	8	A4
Laurelwood Ave.	12	B4
Laverrock Way.	9	E3
Laws Dr.	23	F3
Laws Rd.	23	F3
Lawsondale Ave.	31	G4
Lawsondale Dr.	31	G4
Lawsondale Ter.	31	G4
Lea Rig	30	B3
Leadside Rd.	16	B1
Learney Pl.	11	H2
Leddach Gdns.	30	C3
Leddach Pl.	30	C3
Leddach Rd.	30	C3
Lee Cres.	4	A2
Lee Cres. N.	4	A2
Leggart Ave.	23	E2
Leggart Cres.	23	E2
Leggart Pl.	23	F2
Leggart Rd.	23	E2
Leggart Tce.	23	E3
Lemon Pl.	13	E5
Lemon St.	13	E5
Lerwick Rd.	10	B4
Leslie Cres.	30	C3
Leslie Rd.	12	B2
Leslie Tce.	12	B4
Lethen Wk.	26	A3
Lewis Ct.	10	A5
Lewis Dr.	10	A5
Lewis Rd.	10	B4
Lewisvale.	18	D4
Lickleyhead Way.	3	F2
Liddel Pl.	3	E2
Lilac Pl.	11	F3
Lilybank Pl.	12	B2
Lime St.	17	F1
Lindsay St.	16	D1
Links Pl.	17	F1
Links Rd.	13	F4
Links Rd.	17	G1
Links Rd.	9	G4
Links St.	17	F1
Linksfield Ct.	13	E2
Linksfield Gdns.	13	E3
Linksfield Pl.	13	E3
Linksfield Rd.	13	E3
Lintmill Pl.	10	C2
Lintmill Tce.	10	C2
Lismore Gdns.	10	B5
Little Belmont St.	16	D1
Little Chapel St.	16	C1
Littlejohn St.	12	D5
Livingston Ct.	13	E1
Loanhead Pl.	16	B1
Loanhead Tce.	16	B1
Loanhead Wk.	16	B1
Loch Ct.	12	D5
Loch St.	12	D5
Lochnagar Cres.	18	B3
Lochnagar Rd.	17	G4
Lochnagar Rd.	18	C3
Lochside Ave.	9	E1
Lochside Cres.	9	E1
Lochside Dr.	8	D1
Lochside Pl.	9	E1
Lochside Rd.	9	E1
Lochside Tce.	9	E1
Lochside Way	9	E1
Lochview	30	D2
Lochview Dr.	5	E2
Lochview Pl.	5	E2
Lochview Way.	9	E1
Lock St.	16	D1
Logie Ave.	7	F5
Logie Gdns.	7	F5
Logie Pl.	11	F1
Logie Tce.	11	F1
Loirsbank Rd.	21	F3
Loirston Ave.	25	F4
Loirston Cres.	25	F4
Loirston Manor.	25	F4
Loirston Pl.	17	G4
Loirston Pl.	25	G4
Loirston Rd.	25	G4
Loirston Way.	25	F4
Loirston Wk.	24	A5
Long Walk Pl.	11	E3
Long Walk Rd.	11	E3
Long Walk Tce.	11	E3
Longcairn Gdns.	6	B5
Longlands Pl.	11	E2
Longview Tce.	10	C1
Lord Hay's Ct	9	F5
Lord Hays Grove.	9	F5
Lossie Pl.	10	C4
Louden Pl.	3	E2
Louisville Ave.	15	H4
Lower Denburn	16	C1
Maberly St.	12	C5
Macaulay Gdns.	15	E4
Macaulay Pk.	15	E4
Macaulay Pl.	15	E4
Macaulay Tce.	15	E4
Macaulay Wk.	15	E4
Mackay Rd.	23	F3
MacKenzie Pl.	12	D2
Mackie Pl.	16	B1
Maidencraig Pl.	10	C5
Mains Circ.	31	G3
Mains Ct.	31	G3
Mains Dr.	31	G3
Mains Gdns.	31	G2
Mains View	31	G2
Maitlands Quay	17	F3
Malcolm Pl.	6	D4
Malcolm Rd.	18	A3
Manor Ave.	11	F1
Manor Dr.	7	F5
Manor Pl.	21	F3
Manor Tce.	11	F1
Manor Wk.	11	E1
Manse Rd.	20	D3
Mansfield Pl.	17	F4
Mansfield Rd.	17	G4
Maple Pl.	25	F5
Marchbank Rd.	20	C4
Marchburn Ave.	10	D1
Marchburn Cres.	10	C1
Marchburn Ct. Rd.	10	C1
Marchburn Dr.	10	C1
Marchburn Pl.	10	D1
Marchburn Rd.	10	D1
Marchburn Tce.	11	E1
Marchmont Pl.	24	G5
Marchmont St.	24	G5
Margaret Pl.	16	B5
Margaret St.	16	B2
Marine Ct.	16	D3
Marine Tce.	16	D3
Marischal Ct.	17	E1
Marischal Gdns.	6	B5
Marischal St.	17	E1
Mark Bush Ct.	23	G1
Market La.	12	D2
Market St.	17	E2
Market St.	8	B1
Marlpool Pl.	6	B5
Marquis Rd.	12	A1
Marsh Pl.	26	C3
Martins La.	16	D1
Maryville Pk.	15	F1
Maryville Pl.	15	F1
Marywell St.	16	D2
Mastrick Cose.	11	E4
Mastrick Dr.	10	D4
Mastrick Junction.	10	D4
Mastrick Land.	10	D4
Mastrick Rd.	11	E4
Mathews Quay.	17	F3
Mathews Rd.	23	F3
Mayfield Gdns.	15	G4
McCombies Ct.	16	D1
Meadow Ct.	8	B5
Meadow La.	8	C5
Meadow Pl.	8	C5
Meadowlands Cres.	31	E1
Meadowlands Ct.	31	E1
Meadowlands Dr.	31	E1
Meadowlands Way.	31	F1
Mealmarket St.	13	E5
Mearns Quay.	17	G3
Mearns St.	17	E1
Meikle Gdns.	31	E3
Melrose Wk.	18	B4
Menzies Rd.	17	E4
Merkland La.	13	E3
Merkland Pl.	12	D3
Merkland Rd.	12	D3
Merkland Rd. E.	13	E3
Meston Wk.	12	C2
Mid Chingle Pl.	17	F2
Mid Stocket Mews.	12	A5
Mid Stocket Rd.	15	H1
Middle Brae.	6	A5
Middle Row.	17	H2
Middlefield Cres.	11	G1
Middlefield La.	7	H5
Middlefield Pl.	11	G1
Middlefield Tce.	11	G1
Middlefield Wk.	11	G2
Middlemuir Pl.	6	B5
Middleton Circ.	4	A2
Middleton Cl.	4	C2
Middleton Cres.	4	A2
Middleton Dr.	4	A2
Middleton Grv.	4	A2
Middleton Path.	4	B2
Middleton Pl.	9	E3
Middleton Rd.	4	B2
Middleton Tce.	4	A2
Middleton Way.	4	A2
Midmar Cres.	29	G2
Midmar Pk.	29	G1
Midmar View.	29	G2
Midmar Wk.	29	G1
Migvie Ave.	29	F1
Migvie Gdns.	29	F2
Migvie Grv.	29	F2
Migvie Lea.	29	G2
Mile-End Ave.	12	A5
Mile-End La.	12	A5
Mile-End Pl.	12	A5
Mill Ct.	8	A5
Millarsmires End.	8	C2
Millbank Hse.	16	C3
Millbank La.	12	C4
Millbank Pl.	12	C4
Millburn St.	16	D3
Millden Rd.	21	G3
Milleath Wk.	3	E2
Miller St.	17	E1
Millgrove Rd.	6	C2
Millhill Br.	6	C3
Millside Dr.	18	A4
Millside Rd.	18	A4
Millside St.	18	A4
Millside Tce.	18	A4
Milltimber Br.	19	F3
Miltonfold Ct.	6	C4
Miltonfold.	6	C4
Minden Cl.	9	G3
Minden La.	9	G3
Minster La.	16	C1
Minto Ave.	11	F2
Minto Ave.	24	G3
Minto Dr.	24	G3
Minto Rd.	24	G3
Moir Ave.	11	F2
Moir Cres.	11	F2
Moir Dr.	11	F3
Moir Green	11	F3
Monach Tce.	10	B5
Monearn Gdns.	19	G2
Montgomery Rd.	8	B5
Montrose Cl.	2	A4
Montrose Dr.	22	D2
Montrose Rd.	2	A4
Montrose Way.	2	A4
Monymusk Tce.	14	D3
Moor Pl.	27	E4
Moray Pl.	15	F1
Morgan Rd.	11	H3
Morningfield Rd.	15	G1
Morningside Ave.	22	C1
Morningside Cres.	22	C1
Morningside Gdns.	15	H5
Morningside La.	15	G5
Morningside Mews.	15	G5
Morningside Pl.	22	C1
Morningside Rd.	15	G5
Morrison Dr.	22	B2
Mortimer Dr.	14	C2
Mortimer Pl.	14	C2
Morven Circ.	31	E2
Morven Cres.	30	D3
Morven Ct	17	H4
Morven Dr.	31	E3
Morven Gdns.	31	E3
Morven Pl.	17	F4
Mosman Pl.	11	H2
Moss Side Way.	6	B5
Moss-Side Ct.	31	E5
Moss-Side Pl.	31	E5
Mosside Cres.	26	D3
Mosside Dr.	27	E2
Mount Hooly Way	13	E4
Mount Pleasant.	9	F4
Mount St.	12	B5
Mounthooly.	12	D4
Mugiemoss Ct.	6	D4
Mugiemoss Rd.	6	D4
Muirend Rd.	27	E2
Muirfield Pl.	11	E5
Muirfield Rd.	11	E5
Muirton Cres.	3	F2

38

Mull Way.......... 10 B5
Mundurno Rd...... 8 C2
Murray Ct....... 7 H5
Murray Rd.. 28 D4
Murray Tce....... 16 C4
Murray's La.... 17 E3
Murtleden Rd...... 20 A4
Myrtle Tce.... 26 C2
N St Andrew St... 12 C5
Nellfield Pl....... 16 B3
Nelson La.... 12 D4
Nelson St.... 12 D4
Ness Pl.......... 10 D4
Nether Br....... 6 B5
Nether Kirkgate... 16 D1
Netherby Rd...... 21 E3
Netherhills Ave.... 6 B5
Netherhills Pl.... 6 B5
Netherview Ave... 3 E2
Netherview Pl.... 3 E3
New Pier Rd...... 17 H2
New Pk. Pl....... 10 D4
New Pk. Rd...... 10 D4
Newburgh Circ..... 4 C2
Newburgh Cres..... 8 C1
Newburgh Dr..... 8 C1
Newburgh Path.... 8 C1
Newburgh Pl..... 8 C1
Newburgh Rd..... 4 C2
Newburgh St..... 8 B1
Newburgh Way.... 8 B1
Newhills Ave. 6 B5
Newlands Ave. 15 H5
Newlands Cres.... 15 H5
Newton Pl........ 28 D4
Newton Rd....... 11 F1
Newton Rd...... 2 B3
Newton Rd..... 28 C4
Newton Tce..... 6 D4
Newtonhill Rd..... 28 B4
Newtonvale Ct.... 28 C4
Nicol Pl........ 27 F3
Nigg Kirk Rd...... 24 A2
Nigg Way........ 23 F4
Ninan Pl........ 27 H3
Ninian Rd....... 2 B3
Norfolk Rd...... 15 H5
North Anderson Dr.. 11 F4
North Balnagask Rd.17 H3
North Deeside Rd.. 18 B5
North Donside Rd. . 9 E3
North Esplanade E.. 17 F3
North Esplanade W. 16 D3
North Grampian Circ.. 17 F4
North Silver St.... 16 C1
North Sq........ 17 H2
Northburn Ave..... 15 E2
Northburn La..... 15 E2
Northcote Ave..... 15 E5
Northcote Cres.... 15 E5
Northcote Hill.... 22 E1
Northcote Pk. ... 22 B1
Northcote Rd. ... 22 B1
Northfield Pl..... 16 B1
Northsea Ct...... 13 E1
Novar Pl....... 12 C5
Nursery La...... 11 F3
Oak Cres........ 30 D4
Oak Dr....... 26 D4
Oakdale Tce.... 15 G5
Oakhill Cres.... 15 G1
Oakhill Rd....... 15 G1
Old Skene Rd.... 30 E4
Old Church Rd.... 17 E5
Old Ferry Rd....... 20 C4
Old Meldrum Rd.... 6 D4
Old Mill Rd....... 28 C4

Old Skene Rd..... 29 H5
Oldcroft Ct....... 11 F4
Oldcroft Pl....... 11 F4
Oldcroft Tce....... 11 F4
Oldfold Ave....... 19 F1
Oldfold Cres...... 19 F1
Oldfold Dr........ 19 F1
Oldfold Pk........ 19 G1
Oldfold Pl........ 19 G1
Oldfold Wk........ 19 F1
Old Ford Rd....... 16 D3
Oldmill Rd....... 16 C2
Oldtown Pl........ 10 D1
Oldtown Tce........ 10 D1
Orchard Pl....... 12 D3
Orchard Rd....... 12 D3
Orchard St....... 12 D3
Orchard Wk....... 12 D3
Ord St. 15 E2
Orkney Ave....... 10 A4
Osborne Pl....... 16 A2
Oscar Pl........ 17 F4
Oscar Rd. 17 E4
Overhill Gdns..... 8 C3
Overhills Wk...... 6 A5
Overton Ave....... 3 F4
Overton Circ...... 3 F4
Overton Cres...... 3 F4
Overton Pk........ 3 F4
Overton Way..... 3 F4
Overton Wk....... 3 E4
Oyne Rd......... 14 D3
Palmerston Pl..... 16 D3
Palmerston Rd.... 16 D3
Parade Mews....... 11 F3
Park Br............ 21 F3
Park La.......... 13 E5
Park Pl......... 13 E5
Park Pl......... 28 C5
Park Rd Crt....... 13 E4
Park Rd.......... 13 E5
Park Rd.......... 21 F3
Park Road Ct..... 3 E2
Park St.......... 13 E5
Parkhead Gdns... 6 A5
Parkhill Ave..... 3 E4
Parkhill Circ..... 3 E4
Parkhill Cres...... 3 E4
Parkhill Ct....... 3 E4
Parkhill Way...... 3 E4
Parkside 31 E4
Parkway East..... 9 G2
Partan Skelly Ave.. 25 E4
Partan Skelly Way. . 25 E4
Peacock Ct........ 17 E1
Peat Way........ 27 E3
Penmore Crt....... 5 E1
Pennan Rd........ 8 C5
Pentland Close 17 H3
Pentland Cres.... 17 H4
Pentland Pl...... 17 H4
Pentland Rd....... 17 H3
Peregrine Rd..... 30 C5
Persley Cres...... 11 F1
Perwinnes Path.... 9 E3
Pheonix Pl........ 6 C1
Picardy Ct........ 16 B2
Pilot Sq........... 17 H2
Pinecrest Circ.... 20 B2
Pinecrest Dr...... 20 B2
Pinecrest Gdns.... 20 B2
Pinecrest Wk...... 20 B2
Pinewood Ave..... 14 D4
Pinewood Pl...... 14 D4
Pinewood Pl...... 25 F5
Pinewood Rd..... 14 D4
Pinewood Tce...... 14 D4

Piper Pl.......... 27 G3
Piries Ct......... 12 A1
Piries Lane....... 12 A1
Pitdourie Wk...... 6 B5
Pitfichie Pl....... 3 F2
Pitfodels Station Rd.22 F2
Pitmedden Ave..... 3 E2
Pitmedden Cres... 22 D2
Pitmedden Dr...... 2 D2
Pitmedden Mews.. 2 D1
Pitmedden Rd. .. 2 D2
Pitmedden Rd. .. 22 D1
Pitmedden Tce.. 22 D1
Pitmedden Way... 2 D2
Pitstruan Pl. 16 A4
Pitstruan Tce.. 16 A4
Pittengullies Br... 18 D4
Pittengullies Circ.. 18 D4
Pittodrie La....... 13 E3
Pittodrie Pl....... 13 E3
Pittodrie St....... 13 E3
Plane Tree Rd...... 11 G3
Plover Ct........ 28 D3
Pocra Quay..... 25 G5
Polmuir Ave....... 16 D4
Polmuir Pl....... 16 D4
Polmuir Rd....... 16 D4
Polo Gdns....... 6 C1
Polwarth Rd...... 17 E5
Portal Cres...... 12 C1
Portal Ter....... 12 C1
Portland St. 16 D3
Portree Ave....... 10 B4
Powis Circ....... 12 C2
Powis Cres....... 12 C2
Powis La......... 12 C4
Powis Pl......... 12 C4
Powis Tce........ 12 D3
Poynernook Rd. ... 17 E3
Primrosebank Ave. . 21 G3
Primrosebank Dr. . 21 G3
Primrosehill Ave.. 21 G3
Primrosehill Dr... 21 G3
Primrosehill Gdns. . 12 A2
Primrosehill Pl.... 12 A2
Primrosehill Rd.. 21 G3
Prince Arthur St. . 16 A2
Princes St........ 13 E5
Princess Cres..... 3 F2
Princess Dr....... 3 F2
Princess Pl....... 3 F2
Princess Rd....... 3 F2
Princess Ter...... 3 F2
Princess Walk 3 F2
Princess Way...... 3 F3
Printfield Tce..... 12 A1
Printfield Wk...... 12 A1
Priory Pk........ 18 C4
Privet Hedges...... 11 F3
Promenade Ct..... 13 E2
Promenade Wk 13 E2
Prospect Ct....... 16 D4
Prospect Tce..... 16 D3
Prospect Tce...... 6 C1
Prospecthill Rd. ... 20 C4
Prov Mitchell Circle. 5 E1
Provost Fraser Dr.. 10 D3
Provost Graham Ave. 14 C2
Provost Hogg Ct... 17 G3
Provost Rust Dr... 10 D1
Provost Watt Dr... 23 G1
Puffin Ct........ 28 C3
Quarry Ct........ 20 D3
Quarry Pl........ 10 D2
Quarry Rd........ 10 D2
Quarry Rd........ 20 D3
Quarryhill Ct...... 11 F3

Queen Elizabeth Br. 17 E4
Queen St. 11 H1
Queen St. 17 E1
Queen's Cross. ... 15 H2
Queen's Ct....... 15 G3
Queen's Gate. ... 15 H2
Queen's Gdns. ... 15 H2
Queen's La. N.... 15 H3
Queen's La. S.... 15 H3
Queen's View 10 C1
Queens Ave...... 15 F3
Queens Den...... 14 B1
Queens Rd....... 15 F3
Queens Tce...... 16 A2
Raasay Gdns. 10 B5
Raeburn Pl. 12 C5
Raeden Ave...... 11 G5
Raeden Cres.. ..... 11 F5
Raeden Ct....... 11 F5
Raeden Pk. Rd.... 11 G5
Raeden Pl....... 11 F5
Raeholm Rd...... 8 C2
Raik Rd......... 17 E2
Ramsay Cres..... 22 C1
Ramsay Gdns..... 22 C2
Ramsay Pl....... 22 C2
Rappahouse End... 8 C2
Rattray Pl....... 8 C5
Raxton Pl......... 3 E2
Redmoss Ave..... 24 A4
Redmoss Cres.... 24 A1
Redmoss Pk...... 24 A4
Redmoss Pl...... 24 A3
Redmoss Rd...... 24 A3
Redmoss Tce..... 24 A3
Redmoss Wk...... 24 A3
Redwood Cres.... 25 F5
Regensburg Ct... 10 C4
Regensburg Ct... 10 C4
Regent Ct........ 13 E2
Regent Quay..... 17 E1
Regent Rd....... 17 E2
Regent Wk....... 13 E2
Rennie's Ct..... 16 D1
Rennies Wynd.... 16 D1
Richmond Ct..... 12 B5
Richmond St. 16 B1
Richmond Tce.... 12 B5
Richmond Wk...... 16 B1
Richmondhill Ct... 15 H1
Richmondhill Gdns. 15 H1
Richmondhill Pl. ... 15 G1
Richmondhill Rd. . 15 G1
Ridgeway Grv..... 8 A2
Ritchie Pl........ 8 B5
Riverside Dr..... 16 D5
Riverside Pl..... 23 F1
Riverside Tce.... 16 B5
Riverview Dr....... 3 G3
Robertson Pl..... 19 F3
Robertson Smith Ct. 23 F4
Rockall Pl........ 17 G5
Rockall Rd....... 17 G5
Rocklands Rd..... 21 G2
Ronaldsay Rd..... 10 C5
Ronaldsay Sq..... 10 C5
Rose Hse........ 14 C2
Rose St......... 16 B1
Rosebank Pl..... 16 C3
Rosebank Tce.... 16 C1
Rosebery St...... 11 H5
Rosehill Ave..... 11 H2
Rosehill Cres.... 11 H2
Rosehill Ct...... 11 G3
Rosehill Dr...... 11 H2
Rosehill Pl...... 11 H2
Rosehill Tce..... 11 H2

Street	Page	Grid
Rosemount Pl.	12	B5
Rosemount Sq.	16	B1
Rosemount Tce.	12	B5
Rosemount Viaduct.	16	C1
Rosewell Dr.	15	F1
Rosewell Gdns.	15	E1
Rosewell Pl.	15	E1
Rosewell Tce.	15	E1
Rosewood Ave	24	A3
Roslin Pl.	13	E5
Roslin St.	13	E4
Roslin Tce.	13	E5
Ross Cres.	11	E4
Rousay Dr.	14	C1
Rousay Pl.	14	C1
Rousay Tce.	10	C5
Rowan Ct.	21	F3
Rowan Dr.	30	D4
Rowan Rd.	11	G3
Rowanbank Rd.	27	F3
Royfold Cres.	15	F2
Rubislaw Den Gdns.	15	F2
Rubislaw Den N.	15	G2
Rubislaw Den S.	15	G2
Rubislaw Pk. Cres.	15	F3
Rubislaw Pk. Rd.	15	F3
Rubislaw Pl.	16	A2
Rubislaw Tce.	16	A2
Rubislaw Tce. La.	16	A2
Ruby La.	16	C1
Russell Rd.	17	E2
Ruthrie Ct.	23	E1
Ruthrie Gdns.	22	D1
Ruthrie Rd.	23	E1
Ruthrie Tce.	22	D1
Ruthriehill Rd.	6	B1
Ruthrieston Circ.	16	A5
Ruthrieston Cres.	23	E1
Ruthrieston Ct.	16	A5
Ruthrieston Gdns.	23	E1
Ruthrieston Pl.	16	A5
Ruthrieston Rd.	22	D1
Ruthrieston Tce.	23	E1
Salisbury Pl.	16	A4
Salisbury Tce.	16	A4
Samphrey Rd.	14	B1
Sanday Rd.	15	E1
Sanderling Ct.	28	D3
Sandilands Dr.	12	B1
Scalpay Wk.	10	B5
School Ave.	13	E2
School Cres.	18	C4
School Dr.	13	E2
School La.	18	C4
School Rd.	13	E2
School Rd.	21	F3
School Rd.	18	B3
School Ter.	13	E2
School Wk.	13	E2
Schoolhill	16	D1
Schoolhill Rd.	27	H2
Sclattie Circ.	6	B4
Sclattie Cres.	6	B4
Sclattie Pk.	6	B4
Sclattie Pl.	6	A4
Sclattie Wk.	6	B4
Scotstown Gdns.	9	E4
Scotstown Rd.	8	D1
Scurdie Ness.	24	B5
Scylla Dr.	25	E5
Scylla Gdns.	25	E5
Scylla Grv.	25	E5
Seafield Ave.	15	F4
Seafield Cres.	15	F4
Seafield Ct.	15	F4
Seafield Drive E.	15	F4
Seafield Drive W.	15	F4
Seafield Gdns.	15	F4
Seafield Rd.	15	F4
Seaforth Rd.	13	E4
Seal Craig Gdns.	24	A5
Seamount Rd.	12	D5
Seaton Ave.	13	E1
Seaton Cres.	13	E1
Seaton Dr.	13	E1
Seaton Gdns.	13	E1
Seaton Hse.	13	E1
Seaton Pl.	13	E1
Seaton Pl. E.	13	E1
Seaton Rd.	13	E1
Seaton Wk.	13	E1
Seaview Ave.	5	E1
Seaview Circle.	5	E1
Seaview Cres.	5	E1
Seaview Ct.	13	E2
Seaview Drive.	5	E1
Seaview Pl.	5	E1
Seaview Rd.	9	F4
Seaview Tce.	25	G5
Sedge Pl.	26	C2
Shapinsay Ct.	10	B5
Shapinsay Rd.	10	B5
Shapinsay Sq.	10	B5
Shaw Circ.	30	D3
Sheddocksley Dr.	10	B4
Sheddocksley Rd.	10	C4
Sheildhill Gdns.	25	G4
Sheilhill Gdns.	8	D3
Shepherd Pl.	23	F3
Shetland Wk.	10	B4
Shiprow.	17	E1
Shoe La.	17	E1
Shore Brae	17	E1
Short Loanings.	16	B1
Sillerton La.	23	D2
Silverburn Cres.	9	E2
Silverburn Pl.	9	F2
Silverburn Rd.	8	C2
Silverstone Ct.	22	E2
Simpson Rd.	9	F4
Sinclair Cres.	25	F4
Sinclair Pl.	25	F4
Sinclair Rd.	17	F3
Sinclair Tce.	25	F4
Skateraw Rd.	28	D4
Skelly Rock.	24	G5
Skene House.	16	B2
Skene La.	16	C1
Skene Pl.	2	D3
Skene Sq.	12	C5
Skene St.	16	C1
Skene Tce.	16	C1
Skye Rd.	10	B5
Slains Ave.	8	C2
Slains Cric.	8	C2
Slains La.	8	C2
Slains Pl.	8	C2
Slains Rd.	8	C2
Slains St.	8	C2
Slains Tce.	8	C2
Slessor Dr.	23	F4
Slessor Rd.	23	F4
Sluie Dr.	3	E2
Smithfield Ct.	11	F1
Smithfield Dr.	11	G1
Smithfield La.	7	H5
Smithfield Rd.	11	H1
Smithyhaugh Rd.	10	C1
Society La.	11	H1
Souter Circ.	31	E2
Souter Gdns.	31	E2
Souter Head Rd.	24	B5
South Anderson Dr.	15	H5
South Ave.	21	F3
South Constitution St.	13	E5
South College St.	16	D3
South Crown St.	16	D3
South Deeside Rd.	21	F3
South Deeside Rd.	19	H4
South Esplanade E.	17	F3
South Esplanade W.	17	E3
South Grampian Circ.	17	F4
South Headlands Cres.	28	D4
South Mount St.	12	B5
South Silver St.	16	C1
South Sq.	17	H2
South Stocket Lane	11	F3
South Wk.	11	H3
Southesk Pl.	3	E2
Spa St.	16	C1
Spademill La.	15	G2
Spademill Rd.	15	H2
Spark Tce.	25	G5
Spey Rd.	10	B4
Spey Tce.	10	D4
Spital Wk.	12	D3
Spital.	12	D3
Spring Gdns.	12	D5
Spring Tyne	30	B3
Springbank Pl.	16	D2
Springbank St.	16	D2
Springbank Tce.	16	C3
Springdale Cres.	20	B4
Springdale Ct.	20	B4
Springdale Pk.	20	B4
Springdale Pl.	20	B4
Springdale Rd.	20	B4
Springfield Ave.	15	E3
Springfield Gdns.	15	F4
Springfield La.	15	E3
Springfield Pl.	15	E4
Springfield Rd.	15	F5
Springhill Cres.	10	C3
Springhill Rd.	10	C4
Springhill Tce.	10	C3
Springhill Tce.	25	G5
St Peters Ct.	17	F3
St Andrew St.	12	D5
St Andrew's Tce.	28	B2
St Anne's Cres.	28	B1
St Anne's Wynd	28	C2
St Cathrines Wynd.	16	D1
St Clair St.	12	D5
St Clement St.	17	F1
St Crispin's Rd.	28	B4
St Devenicks Cres.	21	F3
St Devenicks Pl.	21	F3
St Devenicks Tce.	21	G3
St Fitticks Rd.	17	H3
St John's Pl.	16	D2
St John's Rd.	6	D4
St John's Tce.	15	G5
St John's Wlk.	28	C2
St Machar Ct.	8	B5
St Machar Dr.	12	C1
St Machar Pl.	12	D1
St Machar Rd.	12	B2
St Margaret's Pl.	15	E1
St Marys Pl.	16	D2
St Michael's Cres.	28	C3
St Michael's Pl.	28	C3
St Michael's Rd.	28	B2
St Michael's Way.	28	C3
St Michael's Wk.	28	C3
St Nathan's Rd.	28	B3
St Nicholas La.	16	D1
St Nicholas St.	16	D1
St Ninian Ct.	9	F5
St Ninian Pl.	9	F5
St Pauls St.	13	E5
St Peter La.	12	D4
St Peter St.	12	D4
St Peter's Rd.	28	C3
St Peters Tce.	18	B5
St Ronans Circ.	18	C3
St Ronans Cres.	18	D4
St Ronans Dr.	18	C4
St Ronans Pl.	18	D5
St Swithin St.	16	A2
St Ternan's Rd.	28	B4
Stafford St.	12	C4
Stanley Ct.	31	E5
Stanley St.	16	A2
Station Br.	18	C5
Station Rd.	2	D3
Station Rd.	21	G3
Station Rd.	6	C3
Station Rd.	8	A5
Station Rd.	8	A5
Station Rd.	19	F3
Station Rd. E.	18	C5
Station Rd. E.	19	F3
Station Rd. S.	18	B5
Station Rd. W.	18	B5
Stell Rd.	17	E2
Stevenson Ct.	16	C1
Stevenson St.	16	C1
Stewart Cres.	11	E2
Stewart Pk. Ct.	11	G2
Stewart Pk. Pl.	11	G2
Stewart Tce.	11	E2
Sth Constitution St.	13	F5
Stirling St.	16	D4
Stocket Gra.	11	F4
Stocket Parade.	11	F3
Stockethill Ave.	11	F4
Stockethill Cres.	11	F4
Stockethill Ct.	11	F3
Stockethill La.	11	F4
Stockethill Sq.	11	F4
Stockethill Way.	11	F4
Stonehaven Rd.	23	F3
Stoneyhill Tce.	25	G5
Stoneyton Tce.	6	B3
Stoneywood Pk.	3	F5
Stoneywood Pk. N.	3	F5
Stoneywood Rd.	6	C1
Stoneywood Tce.	6	C1
Stornoway Cres.	10	A4
Strachan Pl.	11	F1
Strachan's Mill Ct.	16	C1
Straik Pl.	30	C5
Straik Rd.	30	C5
Strathbeg Pl.	8	D4
Strathburn St.	24	B5
Strathmore Dr.	10	D4
Strawberrybank Parade	16	B2
Stroma Tce.	10	B5
Stronsay Ave.	14	D1
Stronsay Cres.	14	D1
Stronsay Dr.	14	D1
Stronsay Pl.	14	D1
Sugarhouse La.	17	E1
Sumburgh Cres.	10	A4
Summer Pl.	2	D3
Summer St.	12	A1
Summer St.	16	C1
Summerfield Pl.	13	E5
Summerfield Tce.	13	E5
Summerhill Cres.	11	E1
Summerhill Ct.	11	E5
Summerhill Dr.	11	E5
Summerhill Rd.	15	E1
Summerhill Tce.	15	E1
Sunert Rd.	20	A5
Sunert Rd.	19	H2
Sunnybank Pl.	12	C3
Sunnybank Rd.	12	C3

Street	Page	Grid
Sunnybank Wk.	12	C3
Sunnybrae.	6	B5
Sunnyside Ave.	12	C3
Sunnyside Gdns.	12	C3
Sunnyside Rd.	12	C3
Sunnyside Tce.	12	C3
Swannay Rd.	10	B5
Swannay Sq.	10	B5
Sycamore Pl.	16	C4
Tallisman Dr.	22	B2
Tallisman Rd.	22	B2
Tallisman Wk.	22	B2
Tanfield Ave.	12	A1
Tanfield Wk.	12	A1
Taransay Cres.	10	B4
Taransay Ct.	10	B4
Taransay Rd.	10	B5
Tarbothill Rd.	8	D4
Tay Rd.	10	D3
Tedder Rd.	12	C1
Tedder St.	12	C1
Tern Ct.	28	D3
Tern Pl.	5	F2
Tern Rd.	25	E4
Teviot Rd.	10	C4
The Bush.	18	B4
The Chanory.	12	D1
The Courtyard.	30	C4
The Green.	26	C3
The Meadows	19	G1
The Ogilvie Buildings.	16	D2
The Paddock.	18	B5
The Parkway.	8	D2
The Square.	27	E4
TheGreen.	16	D1
Thistle Ct.	16	B1
Thistle Dr.	27	H3
Thistle La.	16	B2
Thistle Pl.	16	B2
Thistle Rd.	2	A4
Thistle St.	16	B2
Thomas Glover Close.	8	D4
Thoms Pl.	12	D2
Thomson St.	12	A5
Thorngrove Ave.	15	G4
Thorngrove Ct.	15	G4
Tillydrone Ave.	12	C1
Tillydrone Ct.	8	C5
Tillydrone Rd.	12	C1
Tillydrone Tce.	12	C1
Tiree Cres.	10	B5
Todhead Gdns.	24	B5
Todlaw Wk.	3	F2
Tollohill Cres.	23	D3
Tollohill Dr.	23	D3
Tollohill Gdns.	23	D3
Tollohill La.	23	D3
Tollohill Pl.	23	D3
Tollohill Sq.	23	D3
Tornashean Gdns.	3	F2
Torry Quay	17	G3
Towerview La.	18	B3
Towerview Pk.	18	B3
Towerview Rd.	18	B3
Towerview Way.	18	B3
Towerview Wk.	18	B3
Trinity Lane	16	D1
Trinity Quay.	17	E1
Trinity St.	16	D1
Tulloch Pk.	6	A5
Tullos Circ.	17	F4
Tullos Cres.	17	F4
Tullos Pl.	17	F4
Turnberry Cres.	8	D2
Turnberry Ct.	8	D2
Turnberry Gdns.	8	D2
Turnstone Ct.	28	D3
Two Mile Cross.	22	D2
Ugie Pl.	10	D4
Uist Rd.	10	A5
Union Bridge.	16	D1
Union Glen.	16	B2
Union Glen Ct	16	B3
Union Gro.	16	A3
Union Gro. La.	16	A3
Union Row.	16	C2
Union Row.	2	D3
Union St.	16	C2
Union Tce.	16	C1
Union Tce. Gdns.	16	C1
Union Wynd.	16	C1
University Cres.	6	B5
University Ct.	6	B5
University Rd.	12	D2
Upper Denburn.	16	C1
Upper Farburn Rd.	2	C4
Upper Mastrick Way.	10	D3
Upperkirkgate.	16	D1
Urquhart La.	13	E4
Urquhart Pl.	13	E4
Urquhart Rd.	13	F4
Urquhart Sq.	13	E4
Urquhart St.	13	E4
Urquhart Ter.	13	F4
Usan Ness.	24	B5
Valentine Cres.	8	B2
Valentine Dr.	8	B2
Valentine Rd.	8	B2
Valley Cres.	23	D2
Valley Gdns.	23	D2
Victoria St.	16	B2
Victoria Br.	17	E3
Victoria Rd.	17	G3
Victoria St.	2	D3
View Tce.	12	B5
Viewfield Ave.	15	F4
Viewfield Cres.	15	F4
Viewfield Crt.	15	F4
Viewfield Gdns.	15	F4
Viewfield Rd.	15	F4
Viking Pl.	27	G3
Villageland Rd.	28	D4
Virginia St.	17	E1
Virginia Ct.	17	E1
Wagley Ct.	6	B5
Wagley Parade.	6	A5
Wagley Pl.	6	B5
Wales St.	13	E5
Walker La.	17	E3
Walker Pl.	17	E4
Walker Rd.	17	E4
Wallace Hse.	14	C2
Wallacebrae Ave.	7	H3
Wallacebrae Cres.	7	H3
Wallacebrae Dr.	7	H3
Wallacebrae Gdns.	7	H3
Wallacebrae Pl.	7	H3
Wallacebrae Rd.	7	H3
Wallacebrae Tce.	7	H3
Wallacebrae Wk.	7	H3
Wallacebrae Wynd.	7	H3
Wallfield Cres.	16	A1
Wallfield Pl.	16	A1
Walton Rd.	2	B3
Walton Rd.	6	A1
Wapping St	16	D2
Wardhead Pl.	10	B4
Watchmans Br.	6	A5
Water La.	17	E1
Waterloo Quay.	17	F1
Waterton Rd.	6	B2
Watson La.	12	B5
Watson St.	12	B5
Waukmill Cres.	10	D1
Waukmill Rd.	10	C1
Wavell Cres.	8	B5
Waverley La.	16	B2
Waverley Pl.	16	B2
Weavers Row.	10	D2
Webster Rd.	23	F3
Weigh-House Sq.	17	E1
Wellbrae Tce.	15	G4
Wellgrove Cres.	30	C4
Wellgrove Dr.	30	C5
Wellgrove Rd.	30	C4
Wellheads Cres.	3	E5
Wellheads Dr.	2	D3
Wellheads Pl.	3	E5
Wellheads Rd.	3	F4
Wellheads Tce.	6	B1
Wellheads Way.	3	E5
Wellington Pl.	16	D2
Wellington Rd.	24	A4
Wellington St.	17	G1
Wellside Ave	29	G1
Wellside Circ.	29	H2
Wellside Cl	29	G1
Wellside End.	29	H2
Wellside Gdns.	29	G1
Wellside Park	29	G1
Wellside Pl	29	G2
Wellside Rd.	29	H2
Wellside Wlk	29	H1
Wellside Wynd	29	H1
Wellwood Tce.	21	G2
West Cairncry Rd	11	F3
West Craibstone St.	16	C2
West Crathie Gdn E.	16	B5
West Crathie Gdn W.	16	B5
West Cults Rd.	21	E3
West Dock St.	17	F2
West Glendale Mews .	16	B3
West Mount St.	12	B5
West North St.	12	D5
West Tullos Rd.	24	A3
Westburn Cres.	12	A4
Westburn Ct.	12	B5
Westburn Dr.	12	A4
Westburn Rd.	12	B5
Westdyke Ave.	30	B4
Westdyke Cl.	30	B3
Westdyke Dr.	30	B4
Westdyke Gdns.	30	B4
Westdyke Pl.	30	C4
Westdyke Tce.	30	B4
Westdyke Way.	30	B4
Westdyke Wk.	30	C4
Westerburn Cres.	12	A4
Western Rd.	12	A1
Westerton Cres.	10	D1
Westerton Pl.	11	E1
Westerton Pl.	21	G3
Westerton Rd.	21	G3
Westfield Gdns.	31	E3
Westfield Rd.	16	A1
Westfield Tce.	16	A1
Westgate.	6	B5
Westhill Cres.	30	D3
Westhill Dr.	31	F3
Westhill Dr.	31	E1
Westhill Gra.	30	C2
Westhill Heights	30	D2
Westhill Rd.	31	H3
Westholme Ave.	15	E2
Westholme Cres. N.	15	E2
Westholme Cres. S.	15	E2
Westholme Tce.	14	D2
Westray Cres.	11	E5
Westray Rd.	10	D5
Westwood Cres.	31	E4
Westwood Dr.	30	D3
Westwood Gro.	30	D3
Westwood Pl.	31	E3
Westwood Way	30	D3
Westwood Wk.	31	E4
Whin Park Gdns.	10	D2
Whin Park Pl.	10	D3
Whin Park. Circ.	26	D3
Whinhill Gate.	16	C4
Whinhill Gdns.	16	C4
Whinhill Rd.	16	C4
Whitehall Mews.	16	B1
Whitehall Pl.	16	A1
Whitehall Rd.	16	A1
Whitehall Tce.	16	A1
Whitehills Cres.	25	E5
Whitehills Way.	25	E5
Whitehouse St.	16	B1
Whiteland Rd.	28	D4
Whitemyres Ave.	11	E5
Whitemyres Pl.	11	E5
Whitestripes Ave.	8	B1
Whitestripes Cl.	8	B1
Whitestripes Cres.	8	B2
Whitestripes Dr.	8	B1
Whitestripes Path.	8	B1
Whitestripes Pl.	8	B2
Whitestripes Rd.	8	B2
Whitestripes St.	8	B1
Whitestripes Way.	8	B1
Wilkie Ave.	11	F1
Willow Wynd.	26	C2
Willowbank Rd.	16	B3
Willowdale Pl.	12	D5
Willowgate Close	16	C3
Willowpark Cres.	11	E5
Willowpark Pl.	11	E5
Willowpark Rd.	11	E4
Windford Rd.	10	C5
Windford Sq.	10	C5
Windmill Br.	16	D2
Windmill La.	16	D2
Windsor Pl.	16	B3
Windyedge Ct.	28	C5
Wingate Pl.	12	C1
Wingate Rd.	12	C1
Wood St.	17	G3
Wood Street Lane	17	G3
Woodburn Ave.	14	D3
Woodburn Cres.	14	D3
Woodburn Gdns.	14	D3
Woodburn Pl.	14	D3
Woodcroft Ave.	4	A1
Woodcroft Grv.	4	A1
Woodcroft Rd.	4	A1
Woodend Ave.	14	C2
Woodend Cres.	14	D1
Woodend Dr.	14	D1
Woodend Pl.	14	D2
Woodend Rd.	14	D1
Woodend Ter.	14	D1
Woodhill Ct.	11	F4
Woodhill Pl.	15	F1
Woodhill Rd.	15	F1
Woodhill Tce.	15	F1
Woodlands Dr.	2	A3
Woodlands Rd.	2	A3
Woodside Rd.	9	F1
Woodstock Rd.	15	G1
Woolman Hill.	16	C1
Wrights Coopers Pl.	12	C1
Wynford La.	31	G3
York Pl.	17	G1
York St.	17	G1
Ythan Rd.	10	C4